Our "Compacted" Compact Clinicals Team

Dear Valued Customer,

Welcome to Compact Clinicals. We are committed to bringing mental health professionals up-to-date diagnostic and treatment information in a compact, timesaving, easy-to-read format. Our line of books provides current, thorough reviews of assessment and treatment strategies for mental disorders. These books will help each practitioner more effectively plan treatment interventions.

We've "compacted" complete information for diagnosing each disorder and comparing how different theoretical orientations approach treatment. Our books use nonacademic language, real-world examples, and well-defined terminology.

Enjoy this and other timesaving books from Compact Clinicals.

Sincerely,

Melanie A. Dean

Melanie Dean, Ph.D.
President

Compact Clinicals Line of Books

Compact Clinicals currently offers these condensed reviews for professionals:

- **Aggressive & Defiant Behavior:** *The Latest Assessment and Treatment Strategies for the Conduct Disorders*

- **Attention Deficit Hyperactivity Disorder (in Adults and Children):** *The Latest Assessment and Treatment Strategies*

- **Borderline Personality Disorder:** *The Latest Assessment and Treatment Strategies*

- **Depression in Adults:** *The Latest Assessment and Treatment Strategies*

- **Obsessive Compulsive Disorder:** *The Latest Assessment and Treatment Strategies*

- **Post Traumatic Stress Disorder:** *The Latest Assessment and Treatment Strategies*

Call for Writers

Compact Clinicals is always interested in publishing new titles in order to keep our selection of books current and comprehensive. If you have a book proposal or an idea you would like to discuss, please call or write to:

Melanie Dean, Ph.D., President
Compact Clinicals
7205 NW Waukomis Suite A
Kansas City, MO 64151
(816) 587-0044

Depression in Adults

The Latest Assessment and Treatment Strategies

Second Edition

by
Anton O. Tolman, Ph.D.

First Edition Titled — Major Depressive Disorder: The Latest Assessment and Treatment Strategies (1995)

Compact Clinicals...*condensed reviews for professionals*

Depression in Adults
The Latest Assessment and Treatment Strategies
Second Edition

by
Anton O. Tolman, Ph.D.

First Edition Titled– Major Depressive Disorder: The Latest Assessment and Treatment Strategies

Published by: Compact Clinicals
                       7205 NW Waukomis Dr., Suite A
                       Kansas City, MO. 64151
                       816-587-0044

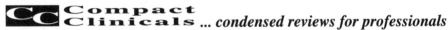

Compact Clinicals *... condensed reviews for professionals*

Copyright © 2001 Dean Psych Press Corp, d/b/a Compact Clinicals

Content Editing by:
    Melanie A. Dean, Ph.D.
Copy Editing by:
    InCredible English
    P.O. Box 1309
    Salt Lake City, UT 84091
DeskTop Publishing by:
    Cactus Tracks
    1958 Five Iron Drive
    Castle Rock, CO 80104
Cover Design by:
    Patrick G. Handley

Library of Congress Cataloging in Publication Data
Tolman, Anton O.
    Depression in Adults: the latest assessment and treatment strategies /by Anton O. Tolman.
        p. ;cm.
    Includes bibliographical references and index.
    ISBN 1-887537-16-3 (pbk.)
        1. Depression, Mental. 2. Depression, Mental--Treatment. I. Title.
    [DNLM: 1. Depressive Disorder--diagnosis. 2. Depressive Disorder--therapy. WM 171
    T652d 2001]
    RC537.T647 2001
    616.85'27--dc21
                                                                00-052312

    ISBN: 1-887537-16-3

                    10 9 8 7 6 5 4 3 2

Read Me First

As a mental health professional, often the information you need can only be obtained after countless hours of reading or library research. If your schedule precludes this time commitment, Compact Clinicals is the answer.

Our books are practitioner oriented with easy-to-read treatment descriptions and examples. Compact Clinicals books are written in a nonacademic style. Our books are formatted to make the first reading as well as ongoing reference quick and easy. You will find:

- *Anecdotes*—Each chapter begins and ends with a fictionalized account that personalizes the disorder. These accounts include a "**Dear Diary**" entry at the beginning of each chapter that illustrates a typical client's viewpoint about their disorder. Each chapter ends with "**File Notes**" of a fictional therapist, Pat Owen. These "**File Notes**" address assessment, diagnosis, and treatment considerations for the client writing the "**Dear Diary**" entries.

- *Sidebars*—Columns on the outside of each page highlight important information, preview upcoming sections or concepts, and define terms used in the text.

- *Definitions*—Terms are defined in the sidebars where they originally appear in the text and in an alphabetical glossary on pages 81 through 82.

- *References*—Numbered references appear in the text following information from that source. Full references appear in a bibliography on pages 83 through 92.

- *Case Examples*—Our examples illustrate typical client comments or conversational exchanges that help clarify different treatment approaches. Identifying information in the examples (e.g., the individual's real name, profession, age, and/or location) has been changed to protect the confidentiality of those clients discussed in case examples.

Contents

Diary of Chris R.

February 10

Finally went to a therapist today. Pat Owen. I guess it's time again; I just seem to be getting worse; can't get up and going. Feels like that black hole again; how I hate that black hole. I'm scared that this time I won't be able to get out of it. It seems hopeless. Dad keeps needing more and more since Mom died. Can't seem to pull myself together to help him. I feel so out of shape, and I need some sleep!

Chapter One: General Information About Depression

Depression is one of the most common mental disorders and has been called the "common cold of psychopathology."[1,2] It is a serious emotional disorder that can range in intensity from mild to severe.

Mild depressive symptoms include sadness, loss of interest in life's activities or pleasure, low self-esteem, changes in sleeping and eating patterns, poor attention and concentration, and a negative outlook on the future. People with mild depression can usually continue work and handle their responsibilities but function below their normal level. These mild depressive symptoms can worsen and lead to a general incapacity to complete work and home responsibilities.

Severe depressive episodes often present additional symptoms of slowed thought and movement, prominent thoughts of guilt, suicidal thoughts and/or plans, and psychotic symptoms (impaired awareness of reality).

Depression is characterized by a persistent disruption in mood with simultaneous interruptions in the person's thoughts, behaviors, and physiological functioning. Social functioning is usually disrupted as well; however, the condition is not diagnosable without significant impairment in major areas of life (e.g., employment, academic, family/marital).

In this book, the term "depression" will refer exclusively to the clinical entity, Major Depressive Disorder in the Diagnostic and Statistical Manual, 4th Edition (DSM-IV).[3] Written for the professional, this book presents:

- General information about Major Depression (in Chapter One)

- Diagnostic information (in Chapter Two)

- Global treatment issues and a discussion of depression's origin (in Chapter Three)

- Psychological treatment approaches (in Chapter Four)

- Biological treatments including medications (in Chapter Five)

This chapter will answer the following:

- *How Common is Major Depression?*—This section gives prevalence rates by percent of people with the disorder and notes the increased prevalence of depression in recent years.

- *What is the Likelihood of Recovery?*—This section discusses recurrence rates and severity as well as the correlation between mortality and depression.

How Common is Major Depression?

Studies show depression to be very common, but how common is difficult to establish. Results of two, large-scale, well-designed studies on the prevalence of depression found that between 5 and 15 percent of Americans suffer from Major Depression at any given time. Similarly, 6 to 17 percent of Americans will suffer from a Major Depressive Episode at some point in their lifetime.[5,6]

Results of prevalence studies consistently indicate that women typically have twice the depression rate of men; although overall, the course of the disorder does not vary by gender. The difference in prevalence rates does not appear to stem from different methods used in different studies.[7] In contrast, prepubescent males and females have the same rate of depression.[8,9,10] Seligman's hypothesis for this discrepancy proposes three possible and compatible explanations:[9]

1. Women are more prone to *learned helplessness* due to various societal factors (see 2 and 3 below). Learned helplessness has been statistically linked to the experience of depression.[11]

2. Given that patterns of negative thinking appear to amplify depression; women's increased tendency toward introspection and *rumination* would make them more likely to become depressed.[10,12]

3. Our society's obsession with equating thinness and ideal beauty affects women more than men. In every culture with this obsession, more women are depressed than men and more women suffer eating disorders. Cultures without the "thin ideal" have equivalent rates of depression for men and women and do not report prevalent eating disorders.[13]

Rates of depression in the United States and western countries appear to be increasing. Early studies demonstrate as much as a 10:1 increase in the rate of depression over the course of the century.[9,15-17]

Based on an approximate U.S. population of 272 million. Fourteen to 40 million women and men are afflicted with depression at any given point in time.[4]

learned helplessness—*learned expectations that one's efforts will have no effect on the outcome*

rumination—*thinking the same thoughts repeatedly*

Seligman[9] also describes a study conducted to predict rates of Depression among seventh graders which found that discontent with developing body shape was a major risk factor for becoming depressed.[14]

As the rate of Depression increases, the likelihood of premature death from suicide will continue to increase, which makes Depression one of the most significant public health problems of the current era.

What is the Likelihood of Recovery?

Recurrent depressive episodes constitute a serious problem; between 50 and 85 percent of those who have an initial depressive episode will have a second one.[18] Individuals with at least two prior episodes are estimated to have a 70 percent chance of a third episode; this peaks at a 90 percent likelihood that those with three prior episodes of depression will have a fourth.[2] A severe first episode of depression appears to predict a recurrent pattern of future depressive episodes, and the presence of chronic physical disorders further increases the likelihood of future depressive episodes. In addition, research indicates that with each recurrent depressive episode, elapsed time between recovery and the next episode decreases, and half of the patients who recover from depression initially are not receiving preventative treatment in the month before they relapse.[19]

Most instances of lifelong recurrent depression co-occur with other psychiatric disorders, often anxiety. These *comorbid* types of depression tend to be more persistent and severe than depression which occurs without other psychiatric disorders.[19]

Probably the most serious complication of depression is suicide (i.e., attempts both successful and unsuccessful). Estimated suicide completion rates are as high as 15 percent among depressed people, a rate that is 3 to 4 times as high as in other psychiatric disorders and 36 times higher than the general population.[20] If, as shown earlier, an average of 10 percent of the population is depressed at any one time, then 4 million people are acting on suicidal plans at any given time. This is very serious when compared to the .00011 percentage of the general population (2,948 people) that commit suicide at any one time (based on information provided by the National Center for Health Statistics).

Depression has widespread health effects; for instance the DSM-IV reports an increased death rate (not necessarily due to suicide) among depressed individuals over 55 years of age. In addition, depressed elderly people admitted to nursing homes have a "markedly increased likelihood of death" in their first year of residence.[3] Some evidence indicates that depression inhibits the immune system, which may relate to increased death rates.[1]

One year after diagnosis of Major Depression, 40% of individuals still have symptoms severe enough to maintain the diagnosis, 20% have some continued symptoms but no longer meet Major Depression diagnostic criteria, and 40% have no mood disorder. Some of these cases, especially mild depressions, subside without treatment.[3]

comorbid—the simultaneous presence of two or more disorders

Risk factors for recurrent depression include:[19]

- *History of multiple depressive episodes*

- *Double depression (experiencing both Major Depression simultaneous with Dysthymia, a chronic form of depression)*

- *Onset of first depressive episode after age 60*

- *Long duration of depressive episodes*

- *Simultaneous presence of anxiety disorders or substance abuse*

*Therapy Notes
From the Desk of
Pat Owen*

Met with C.R. (age 46) today. Complains of poor sleeping, poor eating, missing numerous days of work, sense of inertia in completing family responsibilities. Recent history of maternal death and subsequent increased responsibilities to care for father. Psychiatric history since age 27 when diagnosed with Major Depression. Additional episode since then at age 34. Mixed prognosis given that this appears to be third episode of Major Depression. However, long periods of recovery between episodes and no history of suicide attempts are positive indicators.

Chapter Two: Diagnosing Depression

Diary of Chris R

February 17

Saw Owen today. She wants me to have a complete physical with blood tests. I don't know when I'm going to have time to do that. I know there is nothing physically wrong with me, except that I have gained a lot of weight recently. Dad needs me to take him to the dentist; I feel guilty taking more time off work and feel guilty not being there more for Dad. At least, I should take him to the dentist since I can't seem to help him in any other way. Terry needs me too. I don't think I've been much of a spouse lately. I wish they would all just leave me alone.

What Criteria Are Used to Diagnose Major Depression?

The DSM-IV lists the criteria (Figure 2.1 shown on the next page) for diagnosing a depressive episode.

These criteria are reprinted with permission of American Psychiatric Association, <u>Diagnostic and Statistical Manual of Mental Disorders, Fourth Edition</u>, Washington, D.C., American Psychiatric Association, 1994.[3]

This chapter answers the following:

- **What Criteria Are Used to Diagnose Major Depression?**—This section reviews DSM-IV diagnostic criteria for Major Depressive Disorder.

- **What are Typical Characteristics of Those with Depression?**—This section covers clinical presentation of withdrawn and agitated depression.

- **What Other Depression Types and Classifications Exist?**—This section describes Atypical Depression, Melancholia, Dysthymia and Seasonal Affective Disorder.

- **What Tools Are Available for Clinical Assessment?**—This section covers clinical interviewing, self-report instruments, psychometric assessment of suicide potential, and physiological laboratory findings.

- **What Differentiates Depression from Other Disorders?**—This section helps the therapist differentiate between depression and Bipolar Disorders, Primary Medical Condition, a Substance-Induced Mood Disorder, Dementia, Dysthymia, and Schizoaffective Disorder.

Figure 2.1 — DSM-IV Criteria for Major Depressive Disorder

A. Five (or more) of the following symptoms have been present during the same two-week period and represent a change from previous functioning; at least one of the symptoms is either (1) depressed mood or (2) loss of interest or pleasure.

Note: Do not include symptoms that are clearly due to a general medical condition, or *mood-incongruent delusions* or *hallucinations*.

1. Depressed mood most of the day, nearly every day, as indicated by either subjective report (e.g., feels sad or empty) or observation made by others (e.g., appears tearful).

   Note: In children and adolescents, can be irritable mood.

2. Markedly diminished interest or pleasure in all, or almost all, activities most of the day, nearly every day (as indicated by either subjective account or observation made by others).

3. Significant weight loss when not dieting or weight gain (e.g., a change of more than 5 percent of body weight in a month), or decrease or increase in appetite nearly every day.

   Note: In children, consider failure to make expected weight gains.

4. Insomnia or hypersomnia nearly every day.

5. Psychomotor agitation or retardation nearly every day (observable by others, not merely subjective feelings of restlessness or being slowed down).

6. Fatigue or loss of energy nearly every day.

7. Feelings of worthlessness or excessive or inappropriate guilt (which may be delusional) nearly every day (not merely self-reproach or guilt about being sick).

8. Diminished ability to think or concentrate, or indecisiveness, nearly every day (either by subjective account or as observed by others).

9. Recurrent thoughts of death (not just fear of dying), recurrent suicidal ideation without a specific plan, or a suicide attempt or a specific plan for committing suicide.

B. The symptoms do not meet criteria for a *Mixed Episode*.

C. The symptoms cause clinically significant distress or impairment in social, occupational, or other important areas of functioning.

D. The symptoms are not due to the direct physiological effects of a substance (e.g., a drug of abuse, a medication) or a general medical condition (e.g., hypothyroidism).

E. The symptoms are not better accounted for by bereavement, i.e., after the loss of a loved one, the symptoms persist for longer than 2 months or are characterized by marked functional impairment, morbid preoccupation with worthlessness, suicidal ideation, *psychotic symptoms*, or psychomotor retardation.[3]

mood incongruent—*the content of the delusion (or hallucination) does not match the depression*

delusions—*beliefs strongly held despite contradictory evidence*

hallucinations—*sensory perceptions without external stimulation; hearing voices or seeing things others do not see*

mixed episode—*the person manifests current or past symptoms of* **mania**

mania—*unwarranted euphoria, grandiosity, pressured speech, decreased need for sleep, disturbances of thought processes such as* **circumstantiality**, *and impulsive behavior that often results in negative consequences. (e.g., one-night stands, gambling, speeding, drug use).*

circumstantiality—*manner of talking that is extremely indirect and "circular," tending to talk around a topic*

psychotic (symptoms)—*impairment in awareness of reality, including symptoms of delusions and/ or hallucinations*

Diagnostic Clarifiers

Detailed Specifiers

DSM-IV explicitly endorses a number of more detailed specifiers for current depressive episodes. These specifiers are not coded as such, but enable clinicians to further define the nature and estimate the future course of the disorder. These specifiers include:

- Descriptors of course, such as *"chronic* or *recurrent"*

- Prominent features of the disorder, such as:

  - *Catatonic*

  - *Melancholic*

  - *Atypical*

- Onset of the disorder, such as *postpartum*

Double Depression

According to the DSM-IV, approximately 20 to 25 percent of individuals diagnosed with Major Depression, whether single episode or recurrent, suffer from so-called *"Double Depression."* Both *Dysthymia* and the Major Depression should be diagnosed since each provides significant implications for treatment and prognosis.

Severity of Depression

The clinician must rate the severity of the depression based on the number of symptoms manifested by the client. At one end of the spectrum, those with a minimum of five diagnostic symptoms are given a "mild" rating (as long as functional impairment is considered "minor" by the clinician). Therapists use severe ratings when clients present many more than five symptoms and when the degree of impairment "markedly interferes" with functioning.[3] There are also categories for rating the depression in partial or full *remission* as well as a final "unspecified" category, which remains undefined.

When rating someone's depression as "severe," the therapist must specify whether or not psychotic symptoms of delusions and/or hallucinations are present. If psychotic features are present, the therapist needs to specify whether those features

chronic—*episode has lasted at least two years*

catatonic—*extreme muscle rigidity. Remaining in a fixed state for long periods of time*

melancholic—*worse depression in a.m., early morning awakening*

atypical—*mood brightens at times, excessive sleeping, heavy feeling in arms/legs*

postpartum—*depression occurs within four weeks of having a baby*

double depression—*intense major depressive episode is superimposed upon the milder, chronic depressive disorder called Dysthymia*

Dysthymia—*a persistent, low-level depression that has been ongoing for two years or more*

remission—*absence of all symptoms. Full remission is specified if there have been no symptoms for at least six months, while partial remission indicates no symptoms for less than six months.*

mood congruent–the content of the delusion (or hallucination) matches the depression (e.g., "I am dead.)

are *mood congruent*. When diagnosing "Depression with Psychotic Features," the psychotic symptoms must be secondary to the depression. This means that the psychotic features must have developed after or concurrently with the depressive features.

Recurrent Depression

Recurrent depressive episodes can be given more detailed specifiers of "with or without interepisode recovery" and "seasonal pattern" (e.g., onset and remission of depression at characteristic times of the year, usually beginning in fall or winter and remitting in spring). These specifiers further elaborate on the future course of the disorder.[3]

The therapist must carefully review the client's previous depression history. This review helps ensure accurate diagnosis, assists in considerations of treatment and prognosis, and determines the need for relapse prevention. For example, clients experiencing their second major depressive episode may warrant the expanded diagnosis of "Recurrent Depression." The modifier "recurrent" can be significant because it affects estimates of client prognosis (see chapter 1, page 3).

Diagnostic Challenges

DSM-IV attempts to narrow complex information related to biological, social, and psychological functioning into specific symptom criteria for Major Depression. Because of this complexity, one must be aware of several diagnostic issues, including:[21]

- The symptomatic approach to diagnosis, which requires only a number of specific symptoms to be present to make a diagnosis. This can result in a variety of disorders all being classed as "depression." For example, the DSM-IV has at least 15 types and subtypes of mood disorders leading to over 50 diagnostic code combinations.

- DSM-IV does not include well researched symptoms of depression, such as hopelessness and social withdrawal.

- DSM-IV does not effectively differentiate between depression and grief (the only diagnostic difference being the death of the loved one).

- Some disorders are classified as "adjustment" disorders that seem to have more in common with depression but present less symptoms.

What are Typical Characteristics of Those with Depression?

Depending on the duration, severity, and specific symptoms (e.g., anxiety or psychotic symptoms) of their depression, clients may vary widely in how they present themselves. Of these, depression length and episode severity are the most important factors affecting the presentation. The longer the duration of the depression or the more severe the episode, the more likely the client will display the typical symptoms described below. Clients with "mild" depression probably vary the most in their initial presentation to the clinician while clients suffering from "moderate" to "severe" depression vary less in their presentation and appear more similar to each other.

These general statements about presentation help therapists recognize overt symptoms of depression; individual clients will fluctuate in how well they fit these generalized examples.

The following section describes a typical presentation of depression ("withdrawn" depression) and is followed by a discussion on the less-common, "agitated" type of depression.

Typical Presentation — "Withdrawn" Depression

Many depressed clients manifest feelings (affects), thoughts (cognitions), and behaviors consistent with being sad or withdrawn, such as:

- **Affect**—Depressed clients' emotional display or "affect" may be either *constricted* or *labile*. For example, a depressed patient may smile briefly when asked about past hobbies, but burst suddenly into tears. Clients who are experiencing acute suicidal thinking often appear very tense with tight facial expressions and noticeable tension in their hands, face, or shoulders.

  constricted—the client appears apathetic and does not display much emotion

  labile—marked and rapid mood shifts

- **Cognitions**—Depressed clients often manifest a pessimistic thought pattern. They often discount any positive events in their lives and tend to engage in self-recrimination, criticizing their own behaviors, decisions, or actions. Clients may express feelings of being helpless, powerless, or hopeless.

  cognitions—thoughts

  Aaron Beck and his colleagues point out that there is a typical cognitive triad in the depressed client.[22] This triad involves:

  Aaron Beck—a psychiatrist prominently known for his cognitive behavioral theory and treatments for various mental disorders

  1. A negative view of the self, typically expressed as statements about being defective, deprived, or inad-

The clinician may notice cognitive symptoms of depression such as difficulty concentrating and trouble remembering questions asked. Another prominent symptom may be a slowed mental response time indicated by long pauses before answering questions.

equate. This view may extend to blaming the self as a source of pain to others (e.g., "Everyone would be happier if I were dead.").

2. The tendency to interpret all external events as negative despite plausible alternative explanations (e.g., "The store clerk could see how stupid and slow I am," versus "The store clerk was grumpy with me because he was having a bad day.").

3. A pattern of viewing the future as negative and predicting future failures and disasters (e.g., "I will never be happy in my marriage; I can't get better.").

- **Behaviors**—Depressed clients are often withdrawn and quiet. Voice tone is often soft, making them difficult to hear. They frequently hold their head down, avoid eye contact, and may be seen as being socially isolated. They may not volunteer information about themselves and may frequently respond by saying, "I don't know." They often move slowly, as if they are very tired or in pain, and they may appear indecisive or unwilling to make decisions.

Typical Presentation — "Agitated" Depression

Clients with "agitated" depression tend to show small differences in presentation when compared to clients experiencing "withdrawn" depression. These differences may show up in the client's report rather than be clearly visible. For example, a withdrawn client is more likely to complain of a lack of appetite and of sleeping more than usual. However, an "agitated" client may report overeating, even in the absence of appetite. An "agitated" client may also experience slightly more rumination, which disrupts sleep onset, and may report higher rates of *middle insomnia* as well as *terminal insomnia*.

Those with "agitated" depression manifest affect, cognitions, and behaviors such as:

middle insomnia—waking in the middle of the night with difficulty getting back to sleep

terminal insomnia—waking hours earlier than usual with no return to sleep

- **Affect**—Clients with "agitated" depression often appear preoccupied rather than withdrawn. They are generally tense with either a constricted or labile affect. In contrast to the more "withdrawn" forms of depression, clients with "agitated" depression may often appear angry at themselves or at others. They may express resentment more often than guilt, although both are often present. They may also look as if they feel hurt inside and do not know how to express it.

- *Cognitions*—While clients with agitated depression may still manifest thoughts associated with Beck's Cognitive Triad, their thought patterns focus on being slighted, ignored, or rejected. Clients may be more concerned with how others treat them rather than how they are defective, although themes of self-criticism may also be present. They interpret events around them negatively with an emphasis on how unfair life can be. They also describe high expectations for others as well as themselves and feel hurt or resentful when these expectations are not met. Finally, they may see the future as bleak and actively hostile to their goals.

- *Behaviors*—The most obvious behavior that may be associated with "agitated" depression is increased motor movement. Unlike "withdrawn" clients, who may sit in the same position for the entire session, "agitated" clients may pace in the waiting room, wring their hands, and have trouble remaining seated. Even while remaining seated, they may frequently move their head, arms, or legs. There may be occasional bursts of anger directed toward the clinician (e.g., "I thought I came here for you to give me answers, not for me to answer questions.") These brief outbursts may be followed by contrition or self-blame. They may spontaneously volunteer information about themselves, but can appear impatient with the interview.

What Other Depression Types and Classifications Exist?

In addition to the DSM-IV-defined Major Depressive Disorder, other types and classifications of depression exist, including Atypical depression, Melancholia, Dysthymia, and Seasonal Affective Disorder (SAD).[21]

Atypical Depression

DSM-IV permits the diagnosis of depression with "atypical features" if the core Major Depression criteria are met and the following symptom groups exist:

- Mood brightens in response to actual or potential positive events

- Two of the following exist:
  - ~ Significant weight gain/increase in appetite
  - ~ Hypersomnia
  - ~ Leaden paralysis (heavy feeling in arms or legs)
  - ~ Long-standing interpersonal sensitivity that results in significant social impairment

- Does not meet criteria for catatonic or melancholic features

Atypical depression was initially thought to represent a type of "chronic overreactive dysphoria" and hypersensitivity to disappointment in relationships.

Melancholia

This subtype of depression has long been described as "endogenous," indicating a more biologically based disorder that occurs independent of stressful life events. There is some research support for these assumptions. However, the DSM criteria for melancholic depression have typically changed with each manual edition, leading to some ongoing confusion about the disorder's description. DSM-IV permits classification of a Major Depressive Episode with "melancholic features," which include:

- Either: the loss of pleasure in all or most all activities <u>or</u> the lack of reactivity to usually pleasurable stimuli (does not feel much better when something good happens)

- Plus three or more of the following symptoms:
  - ~ The depressed mood is experienced as distinctly different from the kind of feeling experienced after the death of a loved one.
  - ~ Depression is regularly worse in the morning.
  - ~ The depression sufferer awakens early in the morning (at least two hours before their usual awakening time).
  - ~ The person displays marked psychomotor agitation or retardation.
  - ~ The person suffers from significant anorexia or weight loss.
  - ~ The person experiences excessive or inappropriate guilt.

Dysthymia

This form of depression is less understood than Major Depression. It may often emerge in childhood or adolescence and thus is often integrated into a person's personality development. As a result, those suffering from this long-term, chronic condition tend to have a very pessimistic outlook on life and poor social skills. Treatment implications revolve around helping the person develop a new sense of themselves rather than just returning to a "normal" state. In addition, dysthymia tends to respond poorly to medication treatment and tends toward a long-term course even in psychotherapy. Many individuals with dysthymia may develop Major Depression at some point in their life. Diagnostic criteria for the dysthymia include:

A) The person suffers a depressed mood for most of the day, for more days than not, for at least two years (with the absence of symptoms occurring for no more than two months).

B) The presence of two or more of the following symptoms while depressed:

- Poor appetite or overeating
- Insomnia or hypersomnia
- Low energy or fatigue
- Low self esteem
- Poor concentration or difficulty making decisions
- Feelings of hopelessness

[The disorder is neither better accounted for by chronic Major Depressive Disorder nor occurs exclusively during the course of a psychotic disorder, substance abuse, or a general medical condition.]

Seasonal Affective Disorder (SAD)

The concept of a form of depression that is influenced by climatic elements has been growing in influence in the past decade or more. The essential concept behind SAD is that seasonal fluctuations in the amount of sunlight available may trigger underlying problems with the person's circadian rhythms. Problems with the concept have emerged, however, including the following:

- Seasonal fluctuations may exist in nondepressed populations as well as in depressed populations.
- Within the SAD sufferer's families, there is no elevated prevalence of SAD.
- There is considerable overlap in symptoms between SAD and other types of depression.
- There is a lack of significant evidence for a differential treatment response (early studies showed that photo-therapy or light therapy brought some improvement to persons with nonseasonal depression).
- Individuals with SAD may respond to some traditional antidepressants such as Monoamine Oxidase Inhibitors (MAOI).

DSM-IV permits classification of a SAD if:

A) A regular, temporal relationship exists between the onset of a Major Depressive recurrence and a particular time of the year.

B) Full remissions also occur at a characteristic time of the year.

What Tools are Available for Clinical Assessment?

Diagnosing and assessing depression involves gathering specific information (especially suicide potential) from clinical interviews, self-report instruments, structured interviews, and psychometric assessment instruments.

Clinical Interviewing

During the clinical interview, therapists need to gather information about medical history, family history, and social functioning.

Medical History—Because many medical disorders can mimic or cause depression, the clinician can only diagnose Major Depression if the symptoms are not due to a General Medical Condition.

There are a number of problematic issues that clinicians evaluating clients, who present both with possible depression and a history of medical illness, must consider. These include:[23]

- Possible overlap between vegetative symptoms of illness and depression including fatigue, lack of appetite, and other disturbances of sleeping and eating.

- Some illnesses produce pain and disability, which could be confused with the depression symptoms.

- Depressed mood may directly result from being diagnosed with a life-threatening condition or a disorder (e.g., cancer, heart disease), which could lead to major life changes.

- Some medications or other medical treatments (e.g., chemotherapy) can produce symptoms that appear to be depressive symptoms.

Practically speaking, these issues make the clinician liable for finding out the date of the client's last medical exam and evaluating for the possibility of current medical conditions and treatment. Unfortunately, these tasks are often not part of the typical training program for non-physician, mental health professionals.

If the client is neither being treated for a current medical condition nor has not had a recent physical, the clinician should refer the client for a physical with blood work (ruling out conditions that do not show up routinely in physicals, such as hypothyroidism) and verify that exam results do not account for the depressive symptoms. The clinician can have the client sign a Release of Information form to obtain a copy of the physician's report. In situations where medical conditions are present, the clinician should work with, or consult with, the physician in order to determine how the illness and/or treatments may impact the depression. This may entail discussing the approach taken in psychotherapy and in the medical care, in order to maintain the patient's physical health while reducing the depression. Readers interested in a review of medical conditions presumed to be causally related to depression are referred to the summary by Stevens and colleagues.[23]

Individual and Family Psychiatric History—An assessment of the individual's psychiatric history needs to include questions regarding:

- Recurrent depressive episodes

- Severity of initial episode

The following medical disorders can cause symptoms of depression:

- ***Thyroid disorder*** *often mimics depression (but is also accompanied by dry skin, hair loss, and sensitivity to cold temperatures).*

- ***Diabetic conditions*** *can produce mood swings, depression, irritability, and fatigue.*

- ***Anemia*** *can produce fatigue, sluggishness, and depression.*

- ***Cancer*** *(some forms can produce depression).*

- ***Pre-Menstrual Dysphoric Disorder*** *(formerly Pre-Menstrual Syndrome).*

Studies have indicated that depression occurs 1.5 to 3 times as frequently in first-degree relatives of a depressed individual as in the general population.[3]

- Severity of current episode

- Any previous suicide attempts or thoughts

- Previous psychiatric hospitalization

- Significant stressors (such as childhood abuse, death of a parent, parental divorce)

- Evidence of personality disorder.

The presence of any of these indicators may help confirm the diagnosis and shape the treatment plan.

Because genetics also influence whether or not a person may become depressed, assessment and initial screening of clients presenting for treatment should always include an examination of family psychiatric history, including family history of suicide.

Social Functioning History—Collecting a social and occupational history will help identify any impairment in functioning required to diagnose Major Depression. Ask about school or job performance, socializing, status of friendships, and status of intimate relationships.

Common Predictors Among those who Complete Suicide include:[124]

- *Presence of a Mental Disorder*

- *Psychic Anxiety*

- *Alcoholism and Drug Abuse*

- *Ideas, Discussion, or Preparations for Suicide*

- *Prior Suicide Attempts*

- *Lethality of Method*

- *Anhedonia*

- *Social Isolation*

- *Hopelessness*

- *Attraction to death*

- *Age, Race, and Gender*

- *Genetic and/or Modeling Effects*

- *Problems at Work*

- *Marital Status/Family Factors*

- *Stressors and Life Events*

- *Aggression and Anger*

- *Physical Illness*

- *Comorbidity/Interaction of Specific Predictors*

Suicide Assessment

Given that the presence of depression significantly elevates the risk of suicide, a careful assessment of suicide potential is also part of any routine intake assessment. In evaluating risks, the clinician needs to differentiate between suicide attempts and completed suicides. This distinction is vitally important because 85 to 90 percent of those who attempt suicide never go on to kill themselves. Research indicates the following risk factors for **completed suicide**:[24-26]

1. ***Presence of a Mental Disorder (usually an affective disorder)***—about 15 percent of persons diagnosed with depression eventually commit suicide.

2. ***Psychic Anxiety***—Those who are generally ruminative, anxious, have severe anxiety, or panic attacks, are at greater risk.

3. ***Alcoholism and Drug Abuse***—About 18 percent of all alcoholics eventually kill themselves; the relationship to suicide may be through the disruption in social supports that results from alcoholism.

4. *Ideas, Discussion, or Preparations for Suicide*—As many as 75 to 80 percent of all those who commit suicide give some overt verbal clue to their intentions; clinicians should ask their clients how they would commit suicide or what their plans would be. Those who spend a great deal of time thinking about suicide are at markedly greater risk than those with less suicidal ideation.

5. *Prior Suicide Attempts*—Prior suicide attempts should dramatically raise the level of risk in the clinician's mind; this is especially true for younger females. Older males often succeed on the first try due to the lethality of the method chosen (usually firearms). Clinicians should also determine the person's prior intent during a suicide attempt and assign high risk to those that fully intended and expected to die.

6. *Lethality of Method*—Lethality refers to the probability of a fatal outcome, with quicker methods, such as firearm use, considered more lethal than an overdose. Men typically choose more lethal methods than women, although use of firearms remains the most lethal suicide method of choice by both sexes. Clinicians should routinely assess not only the lethality of current methods planned by the client, but the lethality of the methods used in prior attempts.

7. *Anhedonia*—The loss of pleasure or interest in life and activities.

8. *Social Isolation*—Social contact with others, as long as it is not overtly negative, reduces suicidal potential. Living alone increases suicide potential.

9. *Hopelessness*—Hopelessness may be a better predictor of actual suicides than being depressed. Beck's definition of hopelessness is "inflexible thinking and an inability to consider alternatives to suicide."[27]

10. *Attraction to death*—Positive feelings about death and/or a wish to experience death makes responding to suicidal thoughts easier to act upon.

11. *Age, Race, and Gender*—White males commit 70 percent of suicides, with older, white males having the highest incidence rates. An older, white male who mentions suicide should be taken very seriously.

Specific treatment methodologies for responding to clients who are suicidal are discussed in the section, "How do you Respond to the Inherent Risk of Suicide When Treating People with Depression?" on pages 30 through 32.

Productive employment may buffer people against suicidal tendencies.

12. **Genetic and/or Modeling Effects**—A family history of depression or especially suicide is a strong predictor of suicide.

13. **Problems at Work**—About one-third of those who commit suicide are unemployed at the time of their death; they may also have inconsistent work histories.[128]

14. **Marital Status/Family Factors**—Suicide rates are highest among the divorced and widowed. Family histories of abuse and early disruptions of family life (e.g., frequent moves or death of parent) are related to suicide attempts as an adult.

15. **Stressors and Life Events**—Feelings of worthlessness, shame, guilt, legal problems, loss of close relationships, and chronic overwork are all related to suicide attempts. Most of these stressors are chronic and build up over time; triggering events may be no different than "ordinary" stressors, but may build to the point that the person crosses the threshold of considering suicide.

16. **Aggression and Anger**—Most people who commit suicide are angry in addition to being depressed. They may harbor a desire for "murderous revenge." This is especially prevalent among younger persons. Clinicians should be alert to a history of violence against oneself or others in the assessment.

17. **Physical Illness**—Usually illness by itself is not sufficient to provoke suicidal behavior; however, this can sometimes be a predictor, particularly with cancer, epilepsy, and arthritis.

18. **"Global Insomnia"**—The person experiences difficulty falling asleep, awakens periodically during the night, and wakes early in the morning.

19. **Comorbidity/Interaction of Specific Predictors**—Any one of these listed predictors may be insufficient on its own to produce suicidal behavior. It is more likely that clients will begin to manifest several of these factors at once or over time, even over the course of their life. Clinicians should be aware of the long-term patterns and interactions between specific predictors when making their assessment.

Assessing suicide should involve an "ascending approach," which begins by asking about nonspecific suicidal thinking, then moves into a review of specific passive and active suicidal thoughts.[29] The clinician then asks for a description of all methods the patient has considered and evaluates how much time and effort the patient has expended in considering these suicide plans.

Indicators of acute suicidal ideation that should be considered high risk include:

- Increased patient preoccupation with plan details
- Evidence of scheduling time for planning or for carrying out the plan
- Rehearsal of plan elements
- Experimental action (testing parts of the plan)

The clinician can use checklists during intake procedures to ensure that these important risk factors are evaluated. Once clinicians suspect or confirm suicidal ideation, they should conduct specific evaluations of the client's:

- Suicide plans
- Level of specific detail in those plans
- Lethality of the method being contemplated
- Availability of means to implement the plan
- Proximity of mitigating or helping resources
- The patient's level of self-control

Use of Self-Report Instruments and Structured Interviews

Numerous instruments are available to assist in depression assessment. This section lists those instruments most commonly used and a few others that are relatively new. These instruments fall into five different classes according to how they are administered:

1. Self report instruments
2. Structured interviews
3. Combined instruments
4. Suicide assessment instruments
5. Psychometric instruments

Figure 2.2, on the next page, lists the instruments in these categories; the Appendix offers more detailed information on each.

Figure 2.2 — Depression Assessment Instruments

Type	Use	Instruments Available *For more information on each of these instruments, refer to the Appendix on pages 75-80.*
Self report instruments	Self-report instruments are used to either screen for depression in various settings or to classify subjects for research purposes. They are generally checklists or inventories that are completed by the client.	Beck Cognitive Checklist (CCL) Beck Depression Inventory - 2 (BDI-2) Center for Epidemiological Studies Depression Scale (CES-D) Cornell Scale for Depression in Dementia (CSDD) Geriatric Depression Scale (GDS) Zung Self-Rating Depression Scale (SDS)
Structured interviews	Structured interviews are instruments in which trained clinicians follow a strict interview format that probes for possible symptoms of psychopathology. In some cases, the clinician may be interviewing others (e.g., the Cornell Scale for depression in Dementia); in other cases (e.g., the Diagnostic Interview Schedule or the Composite International Diagnostic Interview), the instrument was explicitly designed so that lay persons could administer the interview.	Composite International Diagnostic Interview (CIDI) Diagnostic Interview Schedule (DIS) Hamilton Rating Scale for Depression (HRSD, sometimes called HAM-D) Schedule for Affective Disorders and Schizophrenia (SADS) Structured Clinical Interview for DSM-IV Axis I Disorders (SCID)
Combined instruments	Combined instruments are those that have an self-report component completed by the client, followed by a semi-structured interview completed by the mental health professional.	Harvard Department of Psychiatry/ National Depression Screening Day scale (HANDS) Prime-MD
Suicide assessment instruments	Instruments specifically targeted for assessing suicide risk.	Beck Hopelessness Scale Beck Scale for Suicide Ideation Firestone Assessment of Self-Destructive Thoughts Suicide Probability Scale
Psychometric instruments	Psychometric assessments are used to facilitate diagnosis and describe personality characteristics.	Minnesota Multiphasic Personality Inventory (MMPI) Rorschach Inkblot Test Thematic Apperception Test (TAT)

Physiological Laboratory Findings

Lab findings, although helpful in continued research regarding the cause or effects of depression on human physiology, do not appear to add precision to diagnostic decisions at this time.

A recent review of potential diagnostic laboratory tests concluded that origins and biology of depression are more complex than was originally thought.[30] Reviewers noted that, in the past decade, no laboratory "gold standard" has emerged for diagnosing depression. Tests previously thought promising, such as metabolites of brain neurotransmitters or the well-known Dexamethasone Suppression Test have largely proven unreliable. Sleep studies need further research but may promise clinical utility in predicting treatment response and monitoring outcome of treatment interventions. Brain imaging techniques, such as CT Scans, may help with differential diagnosis in cases of physiological disorders that mimic apparent depression. However these techniques are still costly and probably should not be considered cost-effective for routine diagnostic use.

What Differentiates Depression from Other Disorders?

When diagnosing Major Depression, the clinician must rule out the possibility that the client's symptoms are related to:

- Bipolar Disorder
- A Primary Medical Condition
- Substance-Induced Mood Disorders
- Dementia
- Dysthymia
- Schizoaffective Disorders

Bipolar Disorders

Clinicians must rule out any previous or current history of mania in a client with depressive symptoms, since depression-specific treatments can sometimes precipitate a manic episode. For example, in a client with a history of mania, lithium has usually been considered the treatment of choice. If a clinician

Laboratory tests used to detect abnormalities include:

- *Sleep and waking EEGs*
- *Measures of neurotransmitter levels or their metabolites in blood*
- *Cerebrospinal fluid, urine, or platelet receptor functioning*
- *Dexamethasone suppression test*
- *Functional and structural brain imaging*
- *Neuroendocrine challenges*
- *Evoked potentials*

unknowingly administered antidepressant medication instead to this person, it could trigger a manic episode. Since those who are manic frequently engage in harmful or destructive behavior toward themselves or others, this is a most important differential diagnosis.

hypomanic—mild mania

Mania is characterized as either a manic episode, mixed episode, or *hypomanic* episode. DSM-IV defines a manic episode as an "abnormally and persistently elevated, expansive, or irritable mood" (p. 328)[3] that has lasted for at least one week unless hospitalization was required during that week. A mixed episode occurs when the client demonstrates both manic and depressive symptoms during the week. Hypomanic episodes share most of the features of manic episodes except that they can have a shorter duration (e.g., four days). In addition, impulsive behaviors seen in hypomania are usually organized, rather than chaotic, and do not usually result in the degree of functional impairment seen in a manic episode. Hypomanic episodes may strain relationships, but do not usually result in hospitalization because these episodes are not usually viewed as destructive.

DSM-IV lists these medical concerns as being related to mood disturbance:[3]

- *Degenerative neurological conditions (e.g., Parkinson's disease, Huntington's disease)*

- *Cerebrovascular disease (e.g., stroke)*

- *Metabolic conditions (e.g., vitamin B1 deficiency)*

- *Endocrine conditions (e.g., hyper- and hypo-thyroidism, hyper- and hypoparathyroidism, hyper- and hypo-adrenocorticism)*

- *Autoimmune conditions (e.g., systemic lupus, erythematosus)*

- *Viral or other infections (e.g., hepatitis, mononucleosis, human immunodeficiency virus [HIV])*

- *Certain cancers (e.g., carcinoma of the pancreas)*

There is a strong link between depressive episodes and mania. According to the DSM-IV, there is a 5-10 percent likelihood that a person having their first depressive episode will later experience a manic episode.[3] Since there is typically no previous history of mania at the time of presentation, clinicians cannot immediately distinguish these individuals from the population of persons suffering only depression. In these cases, the differential diagnosis can only be made over time.

Primary Medical Condition

The clinician needs to determine if depressive symptoms might be related to or caused by a primary medical condition. This differentiation is important for medical professionals to ensure adequate and specific treatment and for non-medical professionals to make appropriate referrals and coordinate care. Between 8 and 10 percent of all depression cases are directly related to a primary medical condition.[31,32] Clinicians should always consider the onset of symptoms and the presence of a known physical disorder, as well as laboratory results and family history. Recommendations for handling medical referrals are reviewed on pages 14-15.

Substance-Induced Mood Disorder

The diagnosis of a Substance-Induced Mood Disorder, new to DSM-IV, involves a disturbance of mood judged by the clinician to be directly related to the physiological effect of a substance (e.g., street drugs, medication, or toxin exposures). For this diagnosis to be made in relation to street drugs there must be evidence of intoxication, withdrawal, or both. For example, cocaine withdrawal may produce depressive symptoms.

The DSM-IV notes that symptoms persisting more than four weeks may indicate mood-related disturbances, rather than substance withdrawal, as substance withdrawal symptoms usually last four weeks or less. DSM-IV also clarifies that some legitimate medications prescribed for other conditions or reasons (e.g., alpha-methyldopa for hypertension or birth-control pills) can either produce depressive symptoms or can exacerbate the course of a preexisting depressive disorder.

Differentiate Substance-Induced Mood Disorder by carefully considering:

- Date of onset (Which condition came first?)

- Drug abuse/dependence history

- Severity of symptoms compared with those expected from intoxication or withdrawal from specific substances

- Prior history of depressive episodes

Differentiating between a primary mood disorder and a substance-induced disorder can be difficult at times given the high propensity with which depressed individuals self-medicate with alcohol or street drugs.

Dementia

Determining whether elderly individuals suffer from depression or Dementia can be difficult because many depressed patients in geriatric settings appear demented (and many of the staff may assume this is the case). Cognitive impairment in these instances is referred to as "pseudo-*Dementia*." Differentiation of these conditions requires clinicians to obtain a good medical history, paying particular attention to personal and family history of Dementia, cancer, stroke, high blood pressure (which can produce strokes or other forms of brain damage), diabetes, and other medical conditions which could produce damage to brain tissue. Carefully assessed functional deficits (e.g., memory loss, sleep or appetite disturbance, loss of grooming or hygiene skills) help determine whether the person has suffered brain damage or if depression is inhibiting their abilities.

Dementia—loss of intellectual capacity in such areas as memory, judgment, and reasoning, usually due to brain deterioration

The therapist should carefully evaluate these functional deficits:

- **Memory Loss**—It is not unusual for depressed elderly patients to display "short-term" memory loss while retaining long-term memory. This short-term loss actually is due to the distractibility or concentration difficulty inherent in cases of depression. Usually Dementia affects long-term memory, as well as verbal or visual memory.

- **Sleep**—Sleep disturbance is common for both Dementia and depression. With depression, the sleep disturbance involves insomnia (often a result of rumination) or excessive sleeping. With Dementia, the sleep disturbance can result from confusion and disorientation about when to go to sleep and where to sleep.

- **Appetite**—Changes in appetite are common with both depression and Dementia. With depression, clients are usually aware of their diminished or increased appetite and will acknowledge this change. With Dementia, changes in appetite or eating patterns often come in the later stages, and the client usually displays little awareness of this change.

- **Grooming or Hygiene Skills**—With both depression and Dementia, these behaviors decrease. However, with depression, poorer grooming skills are related to a loss of motivation to engage in grooming behaviors rather than a loss of skill. With Dementia, people will begin to lose their ability to perform such grooming behaviors as brushing teeth or combing hair. To differentiate between the two during an assessment, the clinician can ask the client to demonstrate "how" to do certain grooming behaviors.

A client with a strong family history of Dementia and no personal or family history of depression should be much more prone to Dementia. However, a client with a history of multiple depressive episodes and long-lived and well-functioning relatives would have a greater likelihood of being depressed.

The therapist should also consider the acuteness of onset. With Dementia, there is typically a gradual deterioration or a step-wise loss of functions (associated with Vascular Dementia). With depression, onset is often abrupt in a person with a good pre-illness history. As with all other differential diagnoses, useful data can come from reviewing family history and previous history of depression.

Dysthymia

dysthymia—a persistent, low-level depression lasting at least two years in an adult

Dysthymia must be distinguished from Major Depression, Chronic type. While both persist over time, Major Depression is much more severe. The symptom list for Dysthymia requires that client presentation meet three of the diagnostic criteria (see page 6), and not include suicidal ideation. Major Depression, Chronic type, requires that the client present with six of the diagnostic criteria, possibly including the more serious suicidal thought patterns. A more detailed description of Dysthymia is included on page 13. It is possible for an individual to suffer from both a Major Depressive episode superimposed upon an existing Dysthymic disorder, resulting in the so-called, "Double Depression."

However, in cases where both disorders may be present, the clinician would not diagnose Dysthymia unless that disorder had been present previous to the onset of the Major Depressive episode. If the client's initial experience was of Major depression, the clinician would not diagnose Dysthymia unless there had been a full remission of the Major Depression (two months of normal mood) prior to onset of the Dysthymia.

While Dysthymia responds well to normal treatments for depression, the course of therapy is often slightly longer, particularly if the Dysthymia has lasted for several years (especially since adolescence). In these cases, clients often incorporate depressive symptoms into their personality style. This occurs because they have no "normal" baseline without the Dysthymia. When clients present symptoms of "double-depression, it is not unusual for them to expect treatment to end when the Major Depressive episode is relieved. At this point, the therapist may discuss treatment options with the client and allow the client to decide the extent of future contact.

Schizoaffective Disorder

In cases of severe depression, psychotic symptoms may be present and may dominate the client's initial presentation. These symptoms may include confused speech, comments about hearing voices, or expressed beliefs that appear to be unfounded (i.e., delusional). These symptoms may obscure an underlying depression.

The difference between a Depressive Disorder with Psychotic Features and Schizoaffective Disorder is that in the latter, psychotic symptoms must occur for at least two weeks without the presence of the depressive symptoms. Additionally, in order to diagnose Schizoaffective Disorder, depressive symptoms must be present more than half of the duration of the illness.

Dysthymia sufferers may present depressive symptoms, but they are often capable of demonstrating a much greater amount of positive affect than those with Major Depression. For example, they may become tearful, but still respond to humor or smile appropriately.

Because clients come to regard the mood disturbance as their "normal" level of functioning, they are often surprised when the clinician informs them that continued treatment can resolve their Dysthymia.

The following example highlights the substantial period of time depressive symptoms can be present during the course of the illness as well as the prominent nature of psychotic symptoms.

Clients with Schizoaffective Disorder might demonstrate prominent psychotic symptoms of delusions and/or hallucinations for two months prior to the onset of Major Depression symptoms. These symptoms might last for three months along with the psychotic symptoms. The depressive symptoms then abate while the psychotic symptoms continue for an additional month.[3]

If the mood disturbance meets criteria for adult Major Depression and is relatively brief compared to the length of the psychotic symptoms, then Schizophrenia and Major Depressive Disorder are diagnosed separately.

*Therapy Notes
From the Desk of
Pat Owen*

Met with C.R. today. No recent physical workup. Recommended one from family physician. She signed release papers for results to be sent to me. Continues to present with constricted affect, feelings of guilt, worthlessness, self criticism. History of depression on maternal side, mother and grandmother. No current suicidal ideation or plans; however, several indicators to watch: recent loss of mother (6 months ago), psychiatric inpatient history, feelings of hopelessness, problems at work (fear of losing job due to excessive absences), and alcohol abuse. No current symptoms of mania or past history of mania. Currently consuming approximately 6-8 oz. of hard liquor daily. Need to assess depressive symptoms following alcohol cessation. Reviewed emergency procedures with C.R. and discussed a "Waiver of Confidentiality" for times of suicidal crisis. Psychological testing scheduled for next week - MMPI-2 and Beck Depression Inventory.

Chapter Three: Global Treatment Issues Related to Depression

Diary of Chris R.

February 24

I am starting therapy with Owen, and I sure hope it helps. I don't know why I feel this way. It seems impossible to pull myself out of this black hole. Maybe it is a "chemical imbalance" as some people say. Maybe medications will help, but I don't like the idea of relying on a pill to feel better. I guess I'll talk to Owen about this and see what she recommends.

This chapter answers the following:

- **What are the Global Treatment Issues Related to Depression?**—This section reviews issues related to the origin of depression; how to respond to suicide potential among those with depression; and general treatment guidelines for depression.

What are the Global Treatment Issues Related to Depression?

Perhaps the most important treatment issue related to depression involves the origin of the disorder. While environmental theorists propose a psychological etiology, success with medications that impact neurochemical functioning supports a biological viewpoint. Recently published work summarizes an integrated position between the two. This section of the book outlines this integrated position and summarizes recent recommendations for treatment.

Another crucial issue for therapists treating clients with depression is the potential for suicide. Therapists have an ethical obligation to plan specific interventions to prevent clients from committing suicide.

What Causes Depression? Is it Due to a Chemical Imbalance, or is it Psychological?

The most frequently asked question about depression is, "What causes depression, a chemical imbalance or psychological processes?" This question stems from the common cultural distinction between emotional/mental processes and physical processes. Medical, psychiatric, and other professional groups have promoted the concept of depression and other mental disorders as a "disease" which lessens social stigma. Unfortunately, this has only increased confusion in the minds of the public and professionals.

Emotions, thoughts, behaviors, and physiology are all manifestations of brain activity directly effected by ongoing social relationships and environmental events. Experimental studies of animal and human learning have clearly indicated that learning produces changes in brain structure, meaning that there are ongoing interactions between brain structure, brain chemistry, and environmental events and relationships. Subsequent chapters in this book will describe unilateral theories of depression's origins from either a psychosocial or a biological perspective. Offering this information will assist readers in understanding the origins of specific treatment methods that evolved from those theories. However, this chapter presents a synopsis of the latest developments in an integrated perspective on the depression's origins, taken mostly from a recently published summary by Sadek and Nemeroff.[33]

In recent years, the most integrated model for understanding depression's origin was the "stress-diathesis" model, which essentially stated that people develop depression (and other mental disorders) as a result of an underlying genetic "predisposition" toward the disorder. According to this model, this predisposition is triggered by environmental events, usually stressful situations or some kind of emotional trauma. In the past two decades, this model has received increasing support, especially as research has demonstrated that previous simple models of depression were unsupported by research. For example, one model not fully supported by research is the biological model that depression is caused by low levels of the neurotransmitters, *norepinephrine* and *serotonin,* in the brain.

nonrepinephrine—type of catecholamine that effects the central nervous system functioning

serotonin—a neurotransmitter from the indoleamin group, which effects central nervous system functioning

Instead, studies have supported the conclusion that the origins of depression are much more complex than previously believed, involving:

- The neurotransmitter systems in the brain

- Alterations in "downstream" receptors of neurotransmitters

- Endocrine and immune system elements, such as cytokines, neuropeptide neurotransmitters (e.g., corticotropin-releasing factor, CRF), thyroid-releasing hormone, somatostatin, and growth hormone releasing factor (GHRF)

Investigators have also realized that while genetic elements clearly play a role in predisposing individuals to depression, they do not follow simple laws of inheritance. These elements are more likely the result of multiple genes interacting; some investigators believe that the contributions of genes to depression may also involve environmental events. Environmental events may trigger or affect the interaction of genes.

Sadek and Nemeroff continue their integration by summarizing research on the human response to stressful events, particularly early physical or sexual abuse trauma.[33] This review clearly indicates the potential for stressful environmental effects to result in substantial changes in brain neurochemistry and structure, including development of a "persistently hypersensitive stress response system." In addition, early trauma may damage or decrease neuron growth in the *hippocampus*, an important brain structure possibly involved with affective disorders.

hippocampus—large, complex, sea-horse shaped brain structure involved in emotion, motivation, learning and long term memory functioning

These early events can then shape an exaggerated response to even mild stress later on in life and lead to depression. Thus, depression presumably occurs in individuals who are genetically vulnerable and who also experience stressful life events as a result of these hypersensitive and over-reactive brain systems. Although not elaborated by Sadek and Nemeroff, brain changes in reaction to the environmental stressors could impact a person's perceptions, thoughts, emotions, and behaviors.

Unfortunately, research demonstrates that this more sophisticated model of the stress-diathesis theory of depression probably does not apply to all individuals who develop depression. Nonetheless, the integrated research described here shows significant promise for improved understanding of what causes depression; it certainly highlights the long-term, damaging effects of physical and sexual abuse. Additionally, this model for understanding depression's origin supports the recommendation for integrated psychological and biological treatments specifically reviewed in chapters four and five respectively.

How Do You Respond to the Inherent Risk of Suicide When Treating People with Depression?

Steps to Take in Managing Suicide Risk:

- *Discuss a waiver of confidentiality for suicide risk*

- *Develop an emergency plan*

- *Establish procedures for inpatient hospitalization*

- *Utilize other interventions with suicidal clients prior to hospitalization*

- *Remove potential instruments of suicide*

- *Make use of psychotropic medications to reduce suicidal risk*

Before beginning to treat depressed clients, the therapist should review the predictors of suicide (see pages 16-18 in chapter 2) and routinely ask clients if they are suicidal or wish to die. If clients give any indication that they have considered suicide in the past or present, the therapist should undertake a careful history of previous ideation, attempts, intent, and methods. In particular, clinicians should ask the clients something like, "If you were going to kill yourself, how would you do it?" The therapist should give consideration to how lethal are the suicide methods that the client reports, the history of past attempts, degree of intent to die, and the clients' access to lethal instruments. For example, in rural areas where hunting is a frequent pastime, it is not unusual for clients to have easy access to firearms. Once clinicians determine that a risk of suicidal behavior exists, they should assess whether the risk is acute, requiring immediate action, or whether the risk would be diminished through outpatient treatment.

If clinicians assess the suicide risk to be manageable through outpatient treatment, experts still urge caution and ongoing reevaluation.

This waiver may offer some legal protection to clinicians who, in good faith, release information in order to protect clients they believe are at serious risk for suicide.

Discussing A Waiver of Confidentiality for Suicide Risk—

Clinicians are urged to discuss a waiver of confidentiality for suicide risk with all clients the first session. This normally consists of advising the client that confidentiality may be waived to protect their safety. The waiver also informs clients that the clinician will take their suicidal thoughts and comments seriously. Clinicians who wish to know more about the potential legal ramifications of a specific waiver should consult an attorney.

Developing an Emergency Plan—All outpatient clinicians
should develop an emergency plan for clients who present with suicidal or even homicidal behaviors. The clinician should discuss this plan with the client early in the first session. Such plans are often provided to the client in written form and make explicit the procedure to follow in an emergency. Although emergency plans vary widely, they often include elements such as calling 911, contacting the

clinician after hours through a phone service or on-call line, or making use of community-based crisis hotlines or hospital emergency rooms.

Establishing Procedures for Inpatient Hospitalization—If the clinician believes there is an imminent risk of suicidal behavior and the client refuses to consider less invasive forms of intervention (described below), the clinician should make arrangements to hospitalize the client. The clinician needs to have prearranged procedures for involuntarily committing a client to a hospital according to state law. Facility selection may depend on the client's insurance benefits and the degree of the client's willingness to be voluntarily hospitalized. Ideally, clinicians should be involved in the ongoing treatment and discharge planning of clients whom they are responsible for hospitalizing.

Utilizing Other Interventions with Suicidal Clients Prior to Hospitalization—A common suicide intervention for clinicians is to specifically ask the client to make a "contract" not to commit suicide. This is often a verbal contract and may be a fairly common procedure in cases where the clinician believes the risk may be minimal or chronic in nature.

In cases where suicide is considered a higher risk, clinicians may want to have the client sign a formal written agreement. This appears to the client as a "serious" promise. If the clinician has reason to believe that the client is not being honest or has broken similar commitments to other therapists, then this procedure will likely have little value. It is not unusual for persons who are at long-term risk of suicidal behavior (particularly those with personality disorders or the chronically mentally ill) to refuse to make such a promise because they have been suicidal most of their life.

Contracts can include clauses that either the client or the therapist will initiate phone contact on a regular basis between sessions to continue the risk assessment and provide some feeling of continuity and connection. This procedure may also increase the chance that the client will become invested in treatment and thus gain a sense of hope.

Removing Potential Instruments of Suicide—At times, clients may be willing to allow a family member or friend to remove potential suicide instruments, thus reducing the risk. For example, a client may permit the clinician to contact a family member or friend to have guns taken away or locked up so that they cannot be used. As Maris notes, the suicidal individual will not automatically find another method.[24]

Increasing the Frequency of Interventions—Clinicians who determine that a suicide risk is moderate, should consider increasing contact frequency with the patient, including increasing the number of sessions per week as well as phone contact in between sessions to check on symptoms and safety.

Using Electro Convulsive Therapy (ECT)—ECT may be an appropriate consideration for patients who express suicidal ideation and refuse to eat. Refer to pages 70-71 for more specific information on ECT.

Involving Other Family Members or Significant Others[34]— Involving family members or other concerned parties to help evaluate and respond to suicide risk can be advantageous. With careful education of the risks involved, the nature of the symptoms, and avenues available to ensure safety (such as hospitalization), involvement of family members may:

- Increase social support for the distressed patient

- Help clinicians gain more information for evaluating ongoing risk

- Provide backup safety options should the suicide risk increase between clinical contacts

Using Psychotropic Medications to Reduce Suicidal Risk— Suicidal clients may respond positively to medications and may be willing to work with a psychiatrist or physician to receive medication that reduces their desire to commit suicide. (See pages 60-67 for the theory and use of *psychotropic medications* in treating depression.) However, clinicians should be aware that many of these medications may take a number of days to work, and for clients at imminent risk, this may not be a safe course to consider. In addition, there are significant numbers of clients who commit suicide using the preventive medication. While this is less of a risk with the newer antidepressant medications, it is a factor that should be considered.

What Are General Treatment Guidelines for Depression?

Recently a number of depression treatment guidelines have been developed based on current research and clinical practice. These guidelines help increase the consistency with which practitioners provide care to depressed clients.[36-41] These recommendations represent the state of knowledge on both biological and psychosocial treatment modalities for depression. Use the preference of the client as a guide to determine which of the following recommendations to adopt:[36]

To reduce the ongoing potential for suicide after the initial suicide crisis:[35]

- *Include the family in treatment.*
- *Realistically inform the patient about probable treatment length and effectiveness as well as expected role of the patient.*
- *Routinely question the patient about suicidal feelings, intent, and plans.*

psychotropic medications—medications that effect behavior, emotions and/or cognitive processes

For Mild-to-Moderate Depression

Use medication or psychotherapy alone. Combined psychotherapy and medication may be indicated if psychosocial issues are important, if there is a history of partial response to only one modality, or if there is a history of poor medication compliance.

For Chronic or Moderate-to-Severe Depression

Use medication either alone or in combination with psychotherapy (unless ECT is planned).[42] Combined medication and psychotherapy would be indicated if there were prominent psychosocial issues, interpersonal problems, a comorbid personality disorder, or a history of poor medication compliance.

The use of ECT should be considered with or without psychotherapy if the depression is severe and any of the following are present: psychosis, patient preference, previous positive response to ECT, need for rapid antidepressant response, or intolerance for medication side effects.

For Psychotic Depression

Use antidepressant medication combined with an antipsychotic medication or ECT.

For All Types of Depression

General treatment guidelines include recommendations made by Beutler and colleagues. These authors reviewed the literature and summarized principles of patient successful change and optimal care, which could be used regardless of professional discipline or theoretical background.[34,42] General principles of practice that produce the best treatment response include:

- Involving others in the therapy, such as family members, spouses, etc., for those clients with complex or chronic histories

- Creating an environment of trust, acceptance, and respect for clients, while using collaborative treatment interventions

- Exposing clients to those behaviors and situations they have been trying to avoid, to stimulate the change process

- Using skill-building and symptom-removal techniques for those clients who externally express their symptoms (e.g. verbalize distress or show irritability, labile affect, or psychomotor agitation)

- Using procedures that emphasize insight and relationships with those clients who tend to internalize their symptoms (e.g. rumination, psychomotor retardation, constricted affect)

- Focusing the initial treatment goals on building new skills and altering symptoms that impact daily functioning

- Using directive interventions for those clients interested in and amenable to treatment

- Using less-directive interventions and possibly paradoxical interventions, such as "authoritatively prescribing a continuation of the symptomatic behavior," for those clients resistant or uninterested in treatment

- Allowing clients to experience emotions in a safe therapeutic environment until they learn to manage those emotions, and their reactions diminish or extinguish

Therapy Notes
From the Desk of
Pat Owen

Today C.R. asked what is causing her depression. I explained that it was interrelated psychological and biological factors. We agreed to proceed with psychological treatment and to start antidepressant medication if she did not respond to psychological treatment as quickly as she would like. She denies suicidal ideation and continues to feel lethargic and hopeless. Plan to meet weekly and evaluate use of medications as an adjunct to psychotherapy in a couple of weeks.

Chapter Four: Psychological Treatments for Depression

Diary of Chris R.

March 24

I have been continuing therapy with Owen. Seems like I'm improving. I feel better. I had never realized how much guilt and unresolved feelings I've carried around about my mother. Maybe it's good that she is dead because I've resolved a lot and can get on with my life, instead of continuing to feel so worthless and trying so hard to please her. Work is much better; I may even get promoted. Ironic, since for awhile, I was sure I was going to lose my job. Terry and I are getting along better, but maybe we need to go to marital therapy like Owen suggested; we still fall into old patterns that make me feel bad. Got to go for now,

Terry and I are playing doubles in tennis tonight.

• **What are the Major Psychological Treatment Methods for Depression?**—*This chapter presents the various theoretical approaches to individual psychotherapy, and research on their effectiveness, for Psychodynamic, Interpersonal Behavioral, Cognitive, and Group Therapies.*

What Are the Major Psychological Treatment Methods for Depression?

As you reviewed in Chapter Three, integrated models of depression's origins emphasize the interactions between environmental and biological factors. This chapter focuses on psychosocial and environmental elements that theoretically contribute to Major Depression and individual treatments associated with each of these approaches:

• **Psychodynamic**—The Psychodynamic approach assumes that historical events and the developmental aspects of personality interact to cause a client's current psychological problems. Some researchers indicate that life ex-

This section examines the following theories regarding environmental causes and treatment of depression:
 • *Psychodynamic*
 • *Interpersonal*
 • *Behavioral*
 • *Cognitive*

periences are the most statistically important influence on depression scores.[43]

- *Interpersonal*—The Interpersonal Therapy (IPT) approach is a modern, short-term, psychodynamic therapy that supports an active role for the therapist and addresses depressive symptoms in relation to current events and relationships. IPT assumes that current social functioning reflects past relationships and that resolving current issues will change interpersonal relationships in the future.

- *Behavioral*—The Behavioral approach focuses on how people's behaviors, specifically social skills, impact their ability to receive *positive reinforcement* from their environment. Since reinforcement increases the measurable frequency of behavior, a person's inability to receive *reinforcement* for healthy behavior directly affects depressive symptoms.

- *Cognitive*—Cognitive theories focus on how the person's internal thoughts, images, and belief systems affect their behavior. While there are several different cognitive theories, treatment methods tend to incorporate behavioral strategies because of the interplay between cognitions and behavior.

positive reinforcement— an event following a person's behavior that increases the frequency of that behavior

reinforcement—any event that increases the frequency of the preceding behavior

What is the Psychodynamic Approach to Treating Depression?

This section highlights two perspectives: classical psychodynamic thought and object relations.

Modern psychodynamic approaches go by several different names, such as Ego Psychology, Object Relations, Psychoanalytic, Psychodynamic, and Neo-Freudian. These schools of thought differ primarily in their theories regarding the role of interpersonal interactions in human personality development. All theories promote the concept that current psychological problems result from historical events.

Psychodynamic Theories—All psychodynamic theorists focus on the development of personality and its interaction with environmental events to explain the origin of depression. In particular, Freud noted that depressed individuals seemed to experience an emotion similar to grief, except that they were more self-judgmental and their self-image tended to be negative. He suggested that contrary to grief, in which a person has experienced an actual traumatic loss of a loved one, the depressed person was suffering from a perceived internal loss to the self.

For example, children who are rejected or ignored by their mother might frequently feel anger or rage at this treatment. As adults, they lose their mother's physical presence, but she is still emotionally present as an internalized representation. In this case, the depressed person's self-criticism reflects an internalized anger toward the abandonment by the mother. Clinicians often call this theory the "anger turned inward hypothesis" of depression.

Object Relations Theorists—More contemporary psychodynamic theorists, most notably those classified as *object relations* theorists, have developed these initial themes in different ways. These theorists refer to the self as the "subject" and other people as "objects." The subject internalizes "objects" and views them within the self as the image or representation of a significant other, most frequently the primary caregiver or "love object."

> **object relations**—"objects" are the internal representation of "others" who are the focus of love or affection. Thus, object relations are the present or past relationships with these internalized love objects.

Blatt, a prominent object relations theorist, also focuses on the theme of loss in the origin of depression.[44] Blatt distinguishes "*anaclitic depression*" from "*introjective depression*," describing how depression develops and manifests itself clinically.

Anaclitic Depression—This type of depression develops when impairment has occurred during the early stage of development, when the child was still in a *symbiotic* relationship with the caregiver and had not yet separated as a distinct identity. As an adult, the person is still stuck at this stage and will fear being abandoned and unloved. Because the person's identity is still at the level of symbiosis, feelings of separateness and anger cannot be expressed directly lest the loved object abandon the person. Consequently, this type of depression is theoretically characterized by feelings of helplessness, weakness, desire to be protected and cared for, and intense fear of loss/abandonment.

> **anaclitic depression**—depressive feelings of abandonment based on the real or perceived loss of one's significant caretaker from childhood

> **introjective depression**—anger turned inward: anger toward one's external parents that couldn't be expressed for fear of rejection and thus results in punitive reactions towards one's self

> **symbiotic**—self and other are perceived as the same (e.g., child sees mother as an extension of self)

The presence of guilt and shame distinguishes anaclitic from introjective depression. Guilt is not part of the pattern for anaclitic depression, because guilt is a result of a later developmental stage in which there are internalized social expectations. Persons at the symbiotic stage of development do not have a conceptualization of others and thus no internalized social expectations, because they perceive everything as happening to themselves.

Introjective depression—In contrast, persons manifesting introjective depression are thought to be past the stage of symbiosis, but have suffered impairment in their ability to separate and individuate from the primary caregiver (love object). As children, when these persons began to separate and act individually from their love object, they came to understand that this separation was not considered good or acceptable by the love object. Thus, as adults, they tend to feel they are unlovable and view resolution of the separation/individuation stage as tantamount to disloyalty; it is "bad" and unworthy of the high ideals which the *superego* imposes on them.

superego—*conscience, internalized societal norms*

The superego in persons with this kind of depression is well developed and is typically harsh, controlling, and committed to high and often unrealistic ideals. For example, such people might be very self-critical if they fail to meet others' expectations, or if they hurt someone else's feelings. They expect themselves to perform at 100 percent without consideration for normal patterns of struggle and conflict in relationships.

Individuals with this type of depression experience intense feelings of guilt, inferiority, and a constant sense of failing others and themselves. They often spend much of their time trying to make up for their failings and are excessively concerned with receiving approval and recognition from the love object since this helps them feel "good" or "worthy."

What Treatment Methods are Used with a Psychodynamic Approach?

Although Object Relations, Ego Psychology, and Neo-Freudian approaches may differ in theory regarding the origin of depression, they are similar in treatment implementation.

The therapist attempts to present a "blank screen" to the client. This represents an attempt to appear neutral and objective, giving no outside direction to the client's thinking. The client projects pressing issues and themes onto a "blank therapist." As the client talks, the therapist listens for current events which reflect the historical conflicts and themes related to the current depressive symptoms.

interpreting—*reflecting to the client a clinical hypothesis regarding the connection between unconscious material and current or conscious material*

catharsis—*allowing the client to experience, in the safety of the clinician's office, the emotion that could not be expressed as a child*

The therapist responds by *interpreting* the client's remarks to help the client achieve insight or understand how developmental patterns shape current responses. The therapist's comments are typically open-ended and vague, allowing the client to further respond without overt direction. The therapist's comments are also directed towards *catharsis*. As clients become aware of these issues, they can integrate this awareness into their ongoing lives and develop into emotionally mature adults.

Throughout the therapeutic sessions, the therapist provides a relationship where the client can openly begin to talk about feeling rejected and being angry without risking another rejection. Using the healing aspect of the therapeutic relationship, the therapist can counter dysfunctional developmental patterns. For example, if the mother was experienced as rejecting or cruel, the therapist creates and nurtures a therapeutic relationship that is safe and allows clients to express themselves without judgment or criticism.

For example, a psychodynamic therapist might sit quietly observing the client who has just come into a session. This client may say, "I just wanted to die after going to the grocery store because no one paid any attention to me. I'm worthless; I'm probably better off dead." As the therapist continues to observe in silence, the client could become angry or even more despondent and say to the therapist, "See, you're doing it, too. I don't even matter enough for you to talk to me." At this point, the therapist could say something like, "Tell me more about feeling rejected." This allows the client to get in touch with these feelings and produce other examples of perceived rejection, all the way back to the primary relationship with the caregiver. At a later time, the therapist could point out the pattern the client has been describing—feeling abandoned and rejected early in life, and then acting in ways now to confirm that rejection, while fearing to overtly express anger at being treated that way.

Clinicians can use the therapeutic relationship to model interpersonal skills for treatment.[45,46] Specifically:

- *Modeling Negotiation Skills*—The therapist expresses views as tentative, open to correction by the client, inviting elaboration and feedback by the client to the therapist. ("It seems like this episode today might be related to how afraid you were to be angry at your mother. What do you think?")

- *Using the "Language Of Mutuality"*—This involves both the therapist and client in a collaboration. ("Can we find other instances when you have felt like telling someone how hurt you were?")

- *Making Statements Rather Than Asking Questions*—This entails offering hypotheses about the client's experiences and how they relate to one another. ("Your feelings of being isolated seem to affect your ability to work with others.")

How Effective is the Psychodynamic Approach in Treating Depression?

Literature cited by noted psychologist Hans Eysenck in a 1991 *meta-analysis* indicated that short-term psychodynamic psychotherapy was no more effective than no treatment at all.[47] This is not a new conclusion. A typical example of this research was a 1979 study involving 178 depressed individuals who were treated with 10 weeks of either insight-oriented psychodynamic psychotherapy, behavioral therapy emphasizing social skills training, Amitriptyline, or relaxation therapy as the control condition. The highest dropout rates in the study were for the psychodynamic and drug therapy conditions. Additionally, researchers found that 30 percent of the clients in the psychodynamic therapy group remained classified as moderately to severely depressed at the end of treatment compared with 19 percent in the control condition. The psychodynamic therapy was rated as the least effective of those used on most outcome measures.[48] Subsequent research has replicated these findings.[49,50]

On the other hand, in another study comparing treatment methods, researchers randomly assigned 117 clients to either an 8- or 16-week treatment protocol with either cognitive-behavioral (CB) or psychodynamic-interpersonal (PI) therapy. The authors of the study emphasized that investigator allegiance was evenly balanced between the two treatment models. Overall results indicated significant improvement in all clients, a result which extended to a 3-month follow-up. Interestingly, researchers found no advantage to a 16-session treatment protocol versus an 8-week protocol. Their results indicated a slight advantage to CB over PI therapy. They concluded that the therapies were equivalent overall, with perhaps a marginal advantage to CB therapy.[45]

Although there is a clear absence of scientific data supporting psychodynamic therapy, this does not necessarily invalidate this treatment.[36,40] This lack of data is partly because such treatments are difficult to standardize and often have deeper therapeutic goals than symptom relief. Overall however, research indicates that modern psychodynamic therapy that is brief, focused, and uses more directive techniques than traditional psychoanalysis appears to be more effective in treating depression than a placebo or no treatment at all.

What is the Interpersonal Therapy (IPT) Approach for Treating Depression?

Interpersonal therapy (IPT) recently gained attention after being included in the National Institute of Mental Health (NIMH) collaborative research program for depression treatment methods.[51] Researchers initially chose IPT as a placebo, but soon found it to be as effective as *tricyclic medications* and cognitive therapy, providing significant relief for up to 70 percent of clients. The assumption behind IPT is that the client's current social functioning reflects past relations. Thus, if the client can resolve current relationship issues, then depressive symptoms ease and changes in interpersonal behavior continue into the future.

tricyclic medications—a class of antidepressant medications effecting all three neurotransmitters. (See pages 60-62 for a detailed discussion of neurological functioning.)

In a recent review, IPT was described as being derived from previous interpersonal and psychobiological theories with an emphasis on the interaction between biological and psychosocial factors in depression.[52] The authors noted that IPT does not endorse a specific model for the cause of depression; however, it does suggest that the patient's interpersonal relationships may be related to the onset of depression and may fuel a depression once it has begun. In contrast to psychodynamic methods, IPT's focus differs in three ways:

1. Clinicians function as active advocates for clients rather than being neutral during sessions.

2. Treatment sessions focus on the "here-and-now" instead of past events.

3. Behavior between client and clinician is explicitly **not** interpreted as *transference*.

transference—the displacing of emotions or attitudes from the client onto the therapist

In IPT, problematic behaviors are determined by early family experiences and participation in early social groups, both of which shape client understanding of social behavior (e.g. the world is a cruel place, so trust no one.) IPT theorists assume that personality plays a role in the development of depression through the way people handle anger, guilt, and overall feelings of self-worth. While theorists see these personality features as part of the predisposing factors in depression, clinical treatment with IPT focuses specifically on understanding symptom development and resolving interpersonal functioning. Clinicians deliberately avoid issues related to personality and psychopathology.

IPT assumes that clinical depression occurs in an interpersonal context and that onset of the disorder, a client's response to treatment, and outcome of therapy are all affected by the quality of the client's interpersonal relationships.

IPT theories emphasize that depression originates with the loss of social attachments; treatment focuses on that loss by:

- Resolving grief issues (e.g., loss of spouse)

- Exploring role transitions (e.g., going from being single to married, from homemaker to employee)

- Addressing maladaptive social behaviors by focusing on social deficits (e.g., lack of eye contact, poor assertiveness skills)

- Resolving previous interpersonal conflict (e.g., defensiveness, inability to communicate clearly)

What Treatment Methods are Used with an Interpersonal Approach?

The usual course of treatment for depression is 12 to 16 sessions with the stated goal of reducing the symptoms of depression while improving the quality of the client's interpersonal functioning.[53,54] Treatment involves three phases: initial, intermediate, and termination.

Assessment focuses on major areas of interpersonal functioning including grief and loss, role transitions, interpersonal conflict, and social skills deficits.

1. **Initial Phase**—This initial phase of treatment usually lasts from one to two sessions. The therapist educates the client about the symptoms and effects of depression, and evaluates the client to determine if medications might be helpful in treatment. The therapist then assesses the client's interpersonal world by reviewing past or current relationships which may be related to the onset of the depressive symptoms and by discussing the changes the client desires in these relationships. In addition, the therapist and client develop an explicit therapy contract with set treatment goals. Finally, the therapist teaches the client the IPT model and discusses practical matters such as fees and scheduling appointments.

One goal in this phase of treatment is to help the client understand the relationship between the depressive symptoms and interpersonal problems.

2. **Intermediate Phase**—In this treatment phase, work begins on the highest priority interpersonal problem area. For example, a client who is recently widowed or divorced may work on either grief, loss, or interpersonal conflict. The experience of losing a loved one may cause role confusion or a loss of part of one's identity. In addition, grief is often related to sadness, anger at the one who died, anxiety about the future, difficulty with concentration, and lack of energy.

The intermediate phase also explores the client's current and past interpersonal relationships to highlight maladaptive patterns. For example, exploring patterns of dependency might reveal how much the client relied on an ex-spouse for instructions and help in social situations. The client could then problem-solve ways to enjoy new independence and gain effective communication skills.

Lastly, treatment in this area seeks to develop new opportunities to grow and form healthy relationships with others (e.g., recently widowed clients who do volunteer work or spend more time with siblings). This phase of IPT treatment typically takes the bulk of the time, lasting from six to eight sessions.

3. **Termination Phase**—The last phase of IPT therapy focuses on preparing the client to complete therapy. Issues include desensitizing the client regarding periods of probable relapse and verifying the option of returning for therapy as needed. In addition, sessions examine plans for continuing to use what was learned in therapy to develop healthy relationships. This phase usually lasts for one to two sessions and completes the course of interpersonal therapy.

Another goal in this phase of treatment is to explore past and current interpersonal patterns and encourage problem-solving to find new ways to resolve old issues.

The therapist reviews treatment goals and progress made toward those goals, determines the client's current assessment of interpersonal relationships, and facilitates the process of saying good-bye to one another.

How Effective is the Interpersonal Psychotherapy Approach in Treating Depression?

IPT has fared very well in studies assessing the utility of psychotherapy in treating depression. The NIMH multi-site collaborative study demonstrated that IPT was at least as effective as antidepressant medications and performed comparably with cognitive therapy. That study demonstrated significant relief for up to 70 percent of clients studied.[51]

Additional studies have supported the efficacy of IPT in randomized, controlled trials.[51,55,56] These studies demonstrated that IPT was superior to antidepressant medication in the treatment of mood, apathy, suicidal ideation, work, and interest measures, while drugs outperformed IPT on vegetative measures (e.g., sleep, appetite, and concentration). At a one-year follow-up, there were no significant differences between psychotherapy and drug treatment across all outcome measures except social functioning. IPT clients continued to demonstrate improvement in social functioning above that found for medicated clients.

In their book, Klerman and Weissman discuss newer applications of IPT to other forms of psychopathology, to groups, and in the treatment of other forms of depression.[53]

In a recent summary of clinical guidelines for treatment, IPT is referred to as one of the approaches with the "…best documented efficiency in the literature for the specific treatment of

major depressive disorder."[36 (pp. 4-5)] These reviewers also noted that IPT may be less effective than Cognitive Therapy for patients with personality disorders and more
effective than Cognitive Therapy for patients with obsessive personality traits or who are single and living alone. Other authors reviewing IPT as a treatment for depression concluded that "...the data regarding IPT as a treatment alone and with antidepressants...are very favorable."[52 (p.234)] They noted that IPT appears to be effective as both an acute and maintenance treatment.

What is the Behavioral Therapy Approach to Treating Depression?

The foundation of behavioral therapy is the concept of reinforcement. Reinforcement increases the frequency of a behavior and is measurable. Since reinforcement increases the rate of behavior, the depressed person either lacks reinforcement for healthy, positive behaviors and/or receives reinforcement for depressive symptoms.

Research has empirically demonstrated that mood varies according to rates of pleasant and aversive activities.

Pleasant activities can serve as a reinforcer in elevating mood. Mood elevates with increases in pleasant activities, but depressed persons often lack the social skills needed for pleasant activities, or at least lack the ability to manifest these skills while they are depressed.[57] Therefore, one main objective of behavioral therapy is to increase the rate of pleasant activities and interactions in order to elevate mood.

Some individuals might feel a substantial elevation in their mood when they are at a party, while others might feel a substantial elevation in their mood when they finish cleaning the garage.

One cannot predetermine what will be reinforcing to a particular client; the only way to tell is to find out whether or not the proposed reinforcer increases the target behavior. For example, praising someone on the job may increase how long that person may stay at work (positive reinforcement), while the same praise may not affect someone else's behavior (no positive reinforcement).

Often, people with depression continue to engage in activities for which few reinforcers are available. For example, a person might work very hard and ignore hobbies or fulfilling interpersonal relationships, but not receive recognition for the extra work. Depressed clients have few reinforcers because of the combination of their own behaviors, their inability to create reinforcing events, and the response of the environment (lack of positive events).

According to behavioral theory, certain reinforcers are thought to be more potent in their effects on mood, but these are highly individualized. For some individuals, the most potent reinforcers are social, while accomplishing tasks may be most potent for others.

At least initially, the expression of depression can be socially reinforced by family and others who attempt to support and encourage depressed persons. Unfortunately, this support can reinforce depressive behaviors, thus increasing their frequency and resulting in an overall decrease in the rate of positive reinforcement from normal life events. For example, when people show initial symptoms of depression (e.g., sadness, some withdrawal), family and friends may rally around and provide support and encouragement. As the symptoms continue, depressed people begin to cut themselves off from pleasant events (e.g., hobbies, friends, or dining out), which were part of their previous normal routines. Family and friends soon tire of giving seemingly futile support, a response viewed as rejection by depression sufferers. Soon, depressed individuals not only lack positive support and encouragement from others, but have very few reinforcers left from their normal routines. This situation increases depression and illustrates the social nature of the disorder.

Unwittingly, the supportive responses of family and friends may reinforce depressive behavior, and the client's depressive behavior may increase in response.

What Treatment Methods are Used with a Behavioral Approach?

Treatment considerations center on the concept that depressed persons can be taught to improve their social skills and increase their participation in pleasant activities. As people begin to experience an increase in pleasant activities and as their ability to relate well to others results in increased social reinforcement for non-depressed behaviors, their depression improves. Therefore, behavioral treatment usually consists of:

- ***Defining a List of Pleasant Events for the Client and Asking Them to Increase the Number of Pleasant Events They Are Doing on a Daily Basis***—This usually entails having clients keep a daily record of their activities, along with pleasure ratings of the activities, from 1 to 10. Pleasant event lists can also be divided into different categories such as social activities and accomplishments, with clients indicating high-reward activities which are singled out for special consideration.

Behavioral treatments for Depression include:
- *Defining a list of pleasant events and deliberately increasing them on a daily basis*
- *Tracking mood by rating mood during events at the beginning and the end of the day*
- *Conducting social skills training*
- *Providing assertiveness training*
- *Building problem-solving skills*
- *Conducting relaxation training*
- *Utilizing behavioral rehearsal and role playing*
- *Practicing "in vivo" exposure*

- *Asking Clients to Track Their Mood by Keeping a Diary of How They Feel During Events, as well as at the Beginning and the End of the Day*—This exercise helps the client and the therapist understand the relationship between mood at the beginning of the day, during activities, and at the end of the day. The mood diary serves as the basis for intervening, with techniques that help increase skills, reinforcers, and consequently mood.

- *Conducting Social Skills Training*—If the client actually lacks social skills, skill training may range from teaching the client how to greet a new acquaintance and shake hands to engaging in relationship-building communication skills.

- *Providing Assertiveness Training*—Assertiveness training focuses on helping clients respond to their own thoughts and feelings without discounting others. Often people with depression feel angry about circumstances over which they have some control.

- *Building Problem-Solving Skills*—This training often accompanies behavioral therapy and includes defining objectives, setting priorities, and analyzing consequences to assist with decision-making.

Ready-made relaxation tapes can be purchased at book stores and practiced at home, or the therapist can make tapes for their clients in which they use their name, unique imagery, and tailored situations.

- *Conducting Relaxation Training*—Depression is usually a very tense state; using techniques such as deep breathing, imagery, and relaxation tapes, can help clients calm themselves in order to respond to situations as they wish. These relaxation skills are incompatible with anxiety-laden, cognitive, and physiological processes. Thus, relaxation skills are often used in conjunction with other specific skills training, such as social skills and assertiveness training.

- *Utilizing Behavioral Rehearsal and Role Playing*—Having clients rehearse and role-play new behaviors during the therapy sessions is often a powerful treatment approach. These techniques allow clients to practice new behaviors and receive direct feedback from the therapist. The therapist and client can then discuss and work on anticipated road blocks to the successful use of new behaviors.

in vivo exposure—with the therapist present, clients practice techniques learned in therapy in the environment that represents the their most feared situation

- *Practicing "In Vivo" Exposure*—*In vivo* exposure is the same thing as actual "on location" exposure. The therapist accompanies the client to an environment typical of a feared social situation. The techniques practiced during the therapy sessions can then be practiced in the actual environment. This allows the client and therapist to perfect the new skills and troubleshoot problems in a safe situation.

How Effective is the Behavioral Therapy Approach in Treating Depression?

Many studies have demonstrated that behavioral treatment of depression can be effective and often superior to other treatments, such as insight-oriented and psychodynamic therapies. In one study, almost 200 outpatients with depression were treated with 10 weeks of behavior therapy, emphasizing skills training in areas like communication, social interaction, assertiveness, and decision-making. Other conditions included a relaxation training control condition, insight-oriented psychodynamic therapy, and antidepressant medication. On outcome measures of depressive symptoms and social adjustment, study results indicated that behavior therapy ranked superior to other conditions on 9 of the 10 measures used. This superiority held up on a three-month follow-up, where behavior therapy was still superior on 7 out of the 10 measures. The insight-oriented treatment group emerged as the worst. Further, unlike the control group, a higher percentage of clients were still classified as moderately to severely depressed in the psychodynamic group.[48] A recent review indicated that:[52]

- Behavior Therapy is often overlooked in recent lists of effective depression treatments .

- Behavioral methods are often included in other forms of therapy (e.g. Cognitive Therapy.)

- Relatively few recent studies have been conducted (e.g., Behavior Therapy was excluded from the NIMH clinical trails already mentioned.)

However, these reviewers noted that Behavior Therapy appears to be effective with depressed patients of all ages; it shows good efficacy, efficiency, and endurance; and they described a recent study that showed equal effectiveness of Behavior Therapy and Cognitive Behavior Therapy.[58] Other authors have noted that Behavior Therapy was generally comparable in efficacy to Cognitive Therapy and pharmacotherapy.[36]

What is the Cognitive Therapy Approach to Treating Depression?

Cognitive theories about the origin of depression appear to fall between psychodynamic and behavioral explanations. This is because they focus on cognitions (thoughts, images) that are internal to depressed persons but affect their behaviors and patterns of social reinforcement. The two most influential of the cognitive theorists are Albert Ellis (Rational Emotive Behavior Therapy) and Aaron Beck (Cognitive Therapy).

What is Rational Emotive Behavior Therapy (REBT)?

Albert Ellis is the founder and preeminent practitioner of REBT. The core concept of REBT is that life events do not drive an emotional disorder. Instead, how a person regards those events can produce emotional and behavioral problems, including depression.

*A*ctivating Events
(situational triggers)

↓

*B*eliefs
(rational & irrational thoughts)

↓

*C*onsequences
(Depression, anger, suicide attempts)

Practitioners describe this theoretical base as the "ABC Theory of Psychopathology" because Activating Events (situational triggers) activate Beliefs (rational and irrational), which are the direct source of emotional and behavioral consequences (e.g., depression, anger, suicide attempt).[59,60]

Ellis states that human beings have inborn, biologically-driven tendencies to experience both rational and irrational beliefs. These beliefs are defined by the impact they have on the individual. Rational beliefs promote a sense of happiness and ability to cope with life, and irrational beliefs promote intense negative emotions that impede the person's ability to deal with life events. In addition, rational and irrational beliefs are distinguished by several other factors.[60] These factors are:

- Verifiability (related to observable data)

- Demandingness (irrational beliefs are rigid and absolute)

- Evaluative conclusions (irrational beliefs produce exaggerated and unrealistic conclusions)

- Behavioral consequences (irrational beliefs produce behaviors that impede ability to function)

A depressed person might believe something that is not based on verifiable or observable data and is rigid and absolute. For example, clients who believe they are unlovable may not allow for those times when parents or friends have been loving toward them. In addition, they may add to this belief by interpreting events in an exaggerated or unrealistic way. For example, a client might decide, "I am unlovable," after going to the store and being virtually ignored by the cashier. Drawing such a conclusion might trigger emotional consequences (such as feeling worthless or suicidal), as well as behavioral consequences (such as attempting suicide or avoiding close friends).

The table below provides examples of rational and irrational beliefs. All the examples are based on the same Activating Event.

Figure 4.1—Activating Event:	The client asks someone she is romantically interested in for a date and gets turned down.
Types of Beliefs	**Beliefs**
Verifiability	
Rational thoughts are observable	He said, "No," to going on a date
Irrational thoughts are unobservable	He hates me.
Demandingness	
Rational thoughts are flexible and malleable	Maybe I'm not his type.
Irrational thoughts are rigid and absolute	Nobody will ever like me.
Evaluative Conclusions	
Rational thoughts produce situation-specific and realistic conclusions	The timing wasn't good for him; maybe he's involved with someone else.
Irrational thoughts produce exaggerated and unrealistic conclusions	I'll never find anybody that will love me.
Behavioral Consequences	
Rational thoughts increase skills and options for behavior	Maybe next time I'll find out more about the person as a friend, then I'll know more about whether or not to ask them out.
Irrational thoughts produce behavior that impedes ability to function	That's it! Trying to make new relationships will never work. I guess I'll have to be alone the rest of my life.

What is Beck's Cognitive Behavior Therapy?

Aaron Beck's cognitive theories of depression are more specifically formulated than those of Ellis. He and his colleagues define a cognitive model of depression that hinges on three major concepts: the cognitive triad, schemata, and errors in judgment or thinking.[22] These concepts are described with examples below:

According to Beck and his colleagues, the symptoms of Depression (ranging from the physiological to considerations of suicide) are consequences of holding negative thought patterns.[22]

The Cognitive Triad—According to Beck, depressed people hold a variety of negative beliefs about:

1. *Themselves*—These beliefs result in self-criticism, guilt, and feelings of worthlessness (e.g., "I should never have left home at 16; I've screwed up my entire life.")

2. *The World Around Them*—Clients expect negative outcomes to their experiences and present others with demands that, because they cannot be met, become barriers to happiness (e.g., "I'll never find a wife; no one will ever want to marry me.")

3. *The Future*—Clients see the future as a bleak place because of anticipated frustration, catastrophe, and pain (e.g., "I'm a failure, so why try; I'll only screw it up.")

Beck's Cognitive model of Depression involves these concepts:
- *The Cognitive Triad*
- *Schemata*
- *Errors in Judgment or Thinking*

Schemata—The concept of *schemata* is important in Beck's work because it links various treatment approaches and is central to understanding personality disorder and depression.[61] Schemata represent underlying cognitive structures that have been built up and elaborated over time, unlike specific negative beliefs usually linked to specific circumstances. These stable patterns of thought can be activated by specific circumstances or triggers and produce consistent response patterns over time.

schemata—belief systems through which events are interpreted

We all use schemata to select information out of the endless stimuli in our environment. However, depressed people use schemata to maintain their negative view of themselves and the world in the face of positive evidence to the contrary. When depressive schemata become activated, they are self-reinforcing because depressed people only notice those events that confirm the negative views and patterns. The stronger schemata become, the less able people are to "switch" them off and activate more reasonable, realistic ways of seeing the world instead. For instance, depressed people with a negative schemata might respond to compliments or praise from others by saying to themselves, "If they really knew me, they'd know

*Beck is careful to point out that he accepts the role of genetics, behavior, and the interpersonal environment in the origin of Depression, but ascribes **primacy**, to the role of thoughts in the generation of depression.[22]*

Schemata can affect not only patterns of thought in the immediate moment, but can actually distort perceptual information.

how close I came to screwing that project up." Thus, the schemata actually distort others' positive remarks and reinforce depressed people's feelings of worthlessness and isolation (e.g., "No one really knows me.").

Errors in Judgment or Thinking—The third concept in Beck's model of depression involves errors in judgment or thinking that occur when negative patterns of thought or schemata are active. These include cognitive distortions and other mistakes in analyzing information, such as:

- *Arbitrary Inference*—"Barbara did not say 'hi' to me this morning; she hates me."

- *Selective Abstraction*—"In talking about our marriage, Bill said he didn't like my cooking; he is so critical of me."

- *Overgeneralization*—"I got a flat tire; my whole life is a disaster."

- *Magnification/Minimization*—"It doesn't matter if people liked my speech."

- *Personalization*—"These layoffs at work are all my fault."

- *Dichotomous (black/white) Thinking*—"I am completely worthless."

These cognitive errors produce intense negative emotional states because they are so rigid, moralistic, and inflexible to changes in the environment.

What Treatment Methods are Used with Cognitive-Behavioral Therapy (CBT)?

Cognitive-behavioral therapists are concerned with identifying, objectively testing, and correcting distorted thought patterns and underlying schemata. Using the active elements in CBT found to be associated with change,[62] a typical treatment method would include these seven phases:

1. *Therapy as Active Collaboration*—From the beginning of treatment, the therapist emphasizes active collaboration with the client and involves the client in setting the agenda for sessions. This is usually done explicitly by asking the client what issues are most pressing and perhaps sharing the therapist's view of what could be accomplished in the session. The client and therapist then mutually agree on which issues to focus during the session.

Arbitrary Inference—jumping to conclusions

Selective Abstraction—only attending to one detail in a series of events or stimuli

Overgeneralization—drawing a general conclusion from a specific incident

Magnification/Minimization—magnifying negatives and minimizing positive situations

Personalization—assuming outside events are related to oneself without evidence

Dichotomous (black/white) Thinking —extremes of idealization/devaluation

The collaboration process immediately involves clients in making decisions and taking charge of their own lives.

This phase involves teaching the client about Depression and the direct role that thoughts can play in improving mood.

2. ***Educate Clients About Depression and the Treatment Approach***—The therapist educates the client about the relationship between events, thoughts, feelings, and behavior, stressing that it is not events themselves that determine emotional reaction, but the thoughts that give the events meaning. (See the ABC model described in the section on Rational Emotive Therapy on pages 48-49.) A client whose relationship is ending might think, "I can never be happy without Marty." The therapist might then use the cognitive triad to point out how such beliefs affect views of oneself, of the world, and the future as well as how this belief contributes to depression. The therapist could then ask the client something like, "What would your life be like if you realized that you could be happy without Marty?" This begins the process of testing the validity of the belief. Typically, CBT therapists elicit more rational thinking from clients through questions which promote other alternatives and a recognition that the target belief was exaggerated (e.g., "Were you ever happy before you met Marty?").

Rational Emotive Therapy has five main steps that parallel the typical CBT treatment method. These are:

1. *Forcefully dispute problematic beliefs*
2. *Engage the client to search for observable evidence to validate beliefs*
3. *Get the client to consider alternative explanations for situations*
4. *Give the client homework*
5. *Utilize in vivo exposure*

3. ***Build Hypothesis-Testing Skills***—The therapist would then teach clients hypothesis-testing skills by first examining specific beliefs that cause emotional distress (e.g., "I can't do anything right."), then directly testing these beliefs (e.g., have the client make lists of what they have done wrong and right over the past three weeks), and asking the client to evaluate the data. This process usually results in a recognition that the belief was absolute or unrealistic and creates the opportunity to make positive change (e.g., "I guess I am right most of the time, but I do make some mistakes.").

4. ***Increase Awareness of Thought Distortions***—This technique helps the client recognize thought distortions (e.g., overgeneralization) when they occur. Therapists use open-ended questions that elicit distorted thoughts and help the client effectively test and eliminate these patterns. In response to a statement like, "I have always been a total failure," the therapist might ask questions like, "Did you fail across the board or were there some areas in which you may have actually done well?" or "Have there been times when some failures have been worse than others? If so, does that mean that the partial failures were also partial successes?"

5. ***Attack Schemata***—When attacking schemata, the therapist should help clients search for contradictory information to the negative schemata content and help them to make more situation-specific conclusions rather than global assumptions (e.g., "I did poorly on that task, but I do better on other tasks." vs. "I am a failure."). Another way to do this is to have clients define qualities (e.g., competence) which are important to them and rate themselves on those qualities on a continuum from total incompetence to complete excellence. Most clients will begin to realize that their competence on different tasks fluctuates and that they are more competent than they originally thought.

6. ***Assign Homework***—Give the client *homework* to focus on therapeutic targets.

   Typical homework assignments involve:

   • Determining which activating events tend to trigger certain beliefs

   • Pinpointing what feelings are attached to particular beliefs

   • Writing down alternate explanations to irrational beliefs

   • Searching for evidence that supports or contradicts certain beliefs

   • Catching "absolute thinking" or "overgeneralizations"

   • Writing down both negative and positive events occurring in their life

7. ***Utilize Behavior Techniques as Necessary***—Add behavioral techniques as necessary and indicated (e.g., increase pleasant events, provide communications and social skills training, use in vivo exposure, and conduct relaxation training).

homework—exercises conducted outside of the therapy session

One example of homework is assigning the client to participate in a "shame attack." This is a term coined by Ellis. The exercise pushes the client to confront their fear and to realize that it is groundless. For example, clients who feel that they have to give in to others might be instructed to deliberately refuse some requests by friends and then to notice that the friendships did not end.

How Effective Is Cognitive Behavior Therapy in Treating Depression?

Both REBT and Cognitive Behavior Therapy (CBT) have been proven highly effective in treating depression. In the original meta-analysis of therapeutic outcome, REBT ranked second in producing the largest improvement in clients among the 10 forms of psychotherapy studied.[63] Another review of 70 REBT outcome studies concluded that after REBT, clients improved significantly compared to those placed on a waiting list for the same amount of time.[64]

Many of the outcome studies in which CBT has been found to be effective are described on pages 67-69 in a summary of comparison studies between psychotherapy and antidepressant medication. Researchers have found CBT to be at least as effective (and sometimes more effective) than medication, especially when relapse and dropout rates are considered. Several meta-analytic studies and other research have concluded that CBT is significantly more effective in treating depression than no treatment and was more effective than other forms of psychotherapy.[51,65,66] Additionally, CBT has been effective in treating "mild" to "severe" depression.[72-74]

A recent review concluded that:[52]

- Beck's CBT is the most extensively evaluated psychosocial treatment for depression.

- CBT may need to be combined with medication for best effectiveness with severely depressed patients.

- To achieve maximal effectiveness, clinicians need to be well trained in CBT due to the treatment complexity.

Other authors noted that Cognitive Therapy has been found equal to or more effective than medications and that the effect of CT has generally been at least as large or larger than other forms of psychotherapy.[36]

How Does Group Therapy Help Those Suffering from Depression?

This section will discuss theory, treatment, and outcome for two major forms of group therapy; cognitive behavioral and interactional/psychodynamic group therapy.

In this era of managed health care and health care reform, using group psychotherapy to treat depression can be cost-effective as well as therapeutically useful. There are well developed guidelines describing the logistics and screening documents used to manage groups.[67,68]

Group therapy is a common form of treatment for depression. Yalom has defined a set of 11 therapeutic factors that probably operate in one form or another in all groups.[67] Some researchers point out that several factors appear especially relevant in the treatment of Major depression. These are Universality, Instillation of Hope, Interpersonal Learning, and Altruism.[69] The following discussion will explain how these and other factors enhance treatment.

- *Universality*—The awareness that other clients suffer similar symptoms and the growing understanding that depression is widespread help to break down the client's feelings of loneliness and isolation.

- *Altruism*—In a group, depressed clients come to realize that they have something to contribute to others. By helping others, they begin to regain a sense of self-worth.

- *Instillation of Hope*—Because hopelessness is a central feature of depression and suicidal ideation, clients in a group witness their peers' progress and learn that depression is not endless. This creates a sense of hope which assists recovery.

- *Interpersonal Learning*—The interpersonal learning that occurs in a group setting challenges the interpersonal struggles inherent in depression. Clients learn how they participate in pushing others away and learn ways to re-connect with peers in the group and (by extension) with important people in their lives outside the group.

How is Group Therapy Utilized to Treat Depression?

Treatment methods discussed in this section focus on cognitive-behavioral group therapy and interpersonal/psychodynamic groups.

Cognitive-Behavioral (CB) Group Therapy—Time-limited and homogeneous groups are the most common among CB therapy groups. In this format, all group members are similarly diagnosed. They begin and end the group simultaneously, and membership is fixed for the duration of the group. These groups are typically time-limited with a specific number of sessions and are highly structured, with therapists playing a directive and active role throughout the therapy.

Early group meetings tend to focus on behavioral techniques designed to increase mood by addressing problems of inertia, passivity, or apathy. This not only improves mood, but as clients begin to experience some successes through the behavioral homework, group leaders challenge thoughts about failure, incompetence, and inability to succeed.

Yalom's Therapeutic Factors of Groups are:[70]
1. *Instillation Of Hope*
2. *Universality*
3. *Imparting Of Information*
4. *Altruism*
5. *The Corrective Recapitulation Of The Family Group*
6. *Development Of Socialization Techniques*
7. *Imitative Behavior*
8. *Interpersonal Learning*
9. *Group Cohesiveness*
10. *Catharsis*
11. *Existential Factors*

The adult course, "Coping with Depression," comes with well-developed manuals for both instructors and participants. The course takes clients through behavioral techniques to improve mood (pleasant events, relaxation) as well as cognitive therapy techniques. Homework assignments are provided and reviewed as part of the treatment.[68]

The therapeutic factor of altruism has an important place in CB groups, namely that as clients help to correct distorted beliefs held by their peers, they are simultaneously correcting and testing their own cognitive distortions.[72]

As the group progresses, therapists give instruction in cognitive therapy with techniques for correcting cognitive distortions. Additionally, the presence of "objective" peers facilitates the testing of distorted beliefs. For example, some clients might believe they are complete failures in life. As group therapy progresses and this belief is uncovered, those clients' peers have the opportunity to argue and test this belief. Feedback from the group that corrects cognitive distortions is of powerful therapeutic value.

Interactional or Psychodynamic Group Therapy—Interactional or psychodynamic groups differ primarily because they function better with clients holding a wide variety of diagnoses. While CB groups are structured and directed by active therapist-leaders, dynamic groups are more loosely structured and would be at risk for "disabling inertia, a failure of spontaneous social interaction, and the possible escalation of symptoms."[69] However, groups with diverse perspectives and defense styles will form their own social system as members interact, and clients will engage in the same interactional patterns that pose problems for them outside the group.

In Psychodynamic Groups, there are no homework assignments or exercises.

Group leaders make use of "here-and-now" interactions to point out interactional patterns to clients and provide opportunities to try new interactive strategies. For example, depressed clients may attach themselves to stronger, protective peers, and they may act in concert during the group. This pattern captures the essence of the depressed person's dependency and unwillingness to be assertive, as well as the protective peer's tendency to dominate others. These patterns can be noticed and discussed in group, allowing insight and encouragement for alternate behaviors.

How Effective is Group Therapy for Treating Depression?

There are few controlled outcome studies on group therapy for depression; however, those conducted have demonstrated that CB groups are superior to placebo or behavior-only therapy conditions.[68,71-74] Recently published guidelines indicate tentative support for Cognitive-Behavioral and Interpersonal group therapies; these guidelines include very limited data suggesting that supportive group therapy might also be useful.[36]

Why is Marital Therapy Used in Treating Depression?

The concept that marital therapy is useful in treating depression may seem controversial. However, both the success of interpersonal treatment and the concept that interpersonal behaviors affect depression support this focus. Some researchers report that the life event that occurred most often prior to the onset of depression, was an increase in arguments with one's spouse.[75] Other authors have found that those with depression are more emotionally vulnerable to hostile comments by family members compared to people with other disorders.[76] Additionally, research indicates a divorce rate nine times higher than that of the general population among those who have experienced a depressive episode.[77]

Studies comparing "normally" distressed spouses with no depression to depressed-distressed couples found that the latter's communication patterns were more erratic and negative. These results suggest that depression and marital distress combine to make the situation worse.[78]

One study found that the lack of an intimate, confiding relationship with a spouse or boyfriend increases a woman's risk of becoming depressed.[79] Further research indicates that those women who reported having marital conflict demonstrated relatively little improvement after individual therapy.[78]

Most studies of marital therapy effectiveness for reducing depression were conducted in the cognitive-behavioral tradition, emphasizing such aspects as communication training and monitoring feedback to each partner. One study comparing antidepressant medication to marital/family therapy showed clients improved earlier with antidepressants. However, this study also showed that marital therapy produced long-term improvements in depression, participation in family role tasks, and increased satisfaction with the marriage.[78]

In a review of marital and family therapy, the authors concluded that Behavioral Couples Therapy (BCT) was as effective as individual Cognitive Therapy in relieving depression symptoms, but was superior to Cognitive Therapy in reducing marital distress.[80] This finding indicates that BCT may be the treatment of choice for depressed patients also experienc-

57

ing marital distress. They also report on Integrative Behavioral Couple Therapy, which extends the behavioral approach by emphasizing spousal acceptance rather than communication skills training. They conclude this new form of marital therapy showed promise. More recent reviews concur with these overall findings.[36]

*Therapy Notes
from the Desk
of Pat Owen*

C.R. is responding well to Cognitive Behavioral Therapy and will recommend treatment of medications in addition. She denies suicidal ideation. Focus in therapy is on resolving irrational beliefs about her caretaking role with father as well as guilt-laden beliefs regarding deceased mother. She is beginning to take more interest in activities as well as focusing on difficulties in her marriage. Recommend marriage therapy for improving communicative and assertiveness skills within that relationship.

Chapter Five: Biological Treatments for Depression

Diary of Chris R.

April 18

I am feeling better but not nearly as well as I want to feel. Progress seems so slow. Maybe I should try medications like Owen suggested. She says it will help me concentrate better and make faster progress in therapy. I'm afraid Terry will think I am weak if I take medication. Also, if I start taking medication maybe I won't ever be able to stop taking them. Owen says that is not true, so maybe I should try it.

This chapter answers the following:

- *What is the Role of Genetics in the Origin of Depression?—This section reviews research indicating a genetic component to depression.*

- *What Neurochemical Influences May Cause Depression?—This section reviews the role of neurotransmitters in the origin of depression.*

- *What are the Major Treatments Methods Used in a Biological Approach?— This section reviews the use of medications to treat depression, research comparing the effectiveness of medications vs. psychotherapy, and other treatments including ECT, St. John's Wort, Exercise and Phototherapy.*

This chapter reviews the genetic and neurochemical (or biological) influences on depression with corresponding medication treatment as well as comparisons of medication to psychological therapies. Other biological treatments are addressed, including the use of Electro Convulsive Therapy (ECT), St. Johns Wort (an herb), exercise, and phototherapy.

What is the Role of Genetics in the Origin of Depression?

Research indicating some genetic basis for depression lends support to the biological viewpoint of the origins of depression.[81] These genetic studies have highlighted that:

- Depression occurs more frequently in first-degree relatives of depressed individuals.

- If one identical twin is depressed, the likelihood that the other twin will also be depressed is significantly higher than for fraternal twins.

Some authors argue that the actual proportion of variability in measures of depression tied to genetic influences is about 16%. They concluded that life experiences were the most statistically important influence on depression scores.[43] Clearly, both genetic and environmental influences are important in understanding the origin of depression.

What Neurochemical Influences May Cause Depression?

As biochemical treatments for depression became more common and effective, researchers began to explore the reasons for their success. This exploration led directly to theories concerning biological influences and highlighted the central role of *neurotransmitters* in depression. The following discussion describes this role.

neurotransmitters—chemical agents that effect behavior, mood, and feelings

Neurotransmitters and depression—To fully understand biochemical theories of depression, clinicians should be aware of current data regarding the role of neurotransmitters in brain functioning.[82-84]

Brain cells, called neurons, constantly transmit information to one another by releasing chemicals into the gap between **neurons**, called the **synapse**. The neuron that releases the chemical is the presynaptic neuron. Cells receiving the chemical message are the postsynaptic cells, which have proteins on the cell surface called **receptors**. Receptors have a specific shape that allows only one molecule of the corresponding pattern to fit, analogous to a key and a lock. When the chemical from the presynaptic cell enters the synapse, it can be picked up by a postsynaptic receptor.

Through a complex system, the postsynaptic cell collates all incoming signals and may fire off a message of its own or may be inhibited from firing a message. The chemical messengers that are transmitted from presynaptic to postsynaptic cells are called neurotransmitters. Since the messengers between cells are chemical, they must either be physically removed from the synapse or destroyed before another message can be sent. The presynaptic cell reabsorbs much of the neurotransmitter that was released, thus clearing the synapse. This process is referred to as **reuptake**.

norepinephrine—a type of catacholamine that effects central nervous system functioning

serotonin—a type of indoleamine that effects the central nervous system

There are also enzymes present in the synapse that will destroy neurotransmitters that are not absorbed through reuptake. These enzymes produce waste products that are referred to as **metabolites**, which are often measured in research studies concerning neurotransmitters and mental illness. Although many neurotransmitters have been identified, the two most important in research concerning depression are *norepinephrine* and *serotonin*.

The classic biochemical theory of depression is called the "*catecholamine/indoleamine*" theory because of the central role of neurotransmitters such as norepinephrine (a catecholamine) and serotonin (an indoleamine).[83,84] The theory stated that depression resulted from depletion or deficiencies of these transmitters in the brain. Monoamine oxidase is one of the enzymes present in the presynaptic terminal which breaks down catecholamines and indoleamines. The MAOI inhibits the action of the enzyme, thus maintaining the neurotransmitter at receptor sites in the postsynaptic neuron. The antihypertensive medication, Reserpine, appeared to deplete the neurotransmitter, leading to depression, while the MAOIs increased neurotransmitter availability, resulting in mood improvements.

A recent review notes that simple depletion of these two neurotransmitters appears to be insufficient for developing depression. Thus, this model of depression is no longer considered adequate.[33] Instead, more complex models represent the current thinking . These models include the role of other neurotransmitters such as Dopamine and highlight the roles and interactions of both the immune and endocrine systems. Chapter 3 presented an integrative model based in current findings.

catecholamine—*a group of neurotransmitters*

indoleamine—*a group of neurotransmitters*

The catecholamine/indoleamine theory was first proposed after clinicians observed that Reserpine, a medication used to treat hypertension, sometimes produced depression as a side-effect. Further research indicated that Reserpine acted to deplete levels of catecholamines in the brain. The monoamine oxidase inhibitor (MAOI), Iproniazid (originally created to treat tuberculosis), was also noted to improve depression in these clients.

What Are the Major Treatment Methods Used in a Biological Approach?

This section covers the use of medications, compares the use of medication versus psychotherapy treatments, and reviews the use of electro-convulsive therapy (ECT), St. John's Wort, exercise, and phototherapy.

What Antidepressant Medications are Used to Treat Depression?

Perhaps the most common form of treatment for depression is the prescription of antidepressant medications. There are several major classes of antidepressant medications including tricyclics and tetracyclics, SSRIs, dopamine-norepinephrine reuptake inhibitors, serotonin-norepinephrine reuptake inhibitors, serotonin modulators, norepinephrine-serotonin modulators, MAOIs, and selective noradrenaline reuptake inhibitors. Figure 5.1 presents a summary of these drug classes and their effects.

Figure 5.1 — Classes and Primary Function of Antidepressant Drugs

Anti-Depressant Class	Function	Remarks
SSRIs	Block serotonin reuptake in the synapse leading to enhanced serotonergic neurotransmission	SSRIs are selective in that they do not usually bind strongly to serotonin receptor sites. Thus, they inhibit serotonin reuptake but only bind weakly to the receptor sites of other neurotransmitters.
Serotonin-Norepinephrine Reuptake Inhibitor [specifically Venlaflexine (Effexor)]	A dual serotonin/norepinephrine reuptake inhibitor that can be thought of as a tricyclic antidepressant without the negative side effects of the tricyclics[85]	Venlaxafine is reported to be very effective in treating depression, particularly with patients who have failed to respond to other antidepressants, including the SSRIs. It also appears to be more effective than the SSRIs in the treatment of severe depression and may have a more rapid onset of action than other antidepressants.[85]
Dopamine-Norepinephrine Reuptake Inhibitor [specifically Buproprion}	Blocks the reuptake of dopamine and norepinephrine in the synapse	
Selective Noradrenaline Reuptake Inhibitor [specifically Reboxetine (Edronax, Vestra)]	Selectively inhibits the reuptake of norepinephrine	Currently pending expected U.S. FDA approval but has been approved for use in Europe for several years. Reboxetine has been shown to be more effective than placebo and appears to be at least as effective as tricyclic agents.[36]
Serotonin modulators [specifically Nefazodone (Serzone) and Trazodone]	Inhibit presynaptic serotonin reuptake and block postsynaptic serotonin receptors	These medications preserve normal sleep patterns and avoid the sexual side effects that often accompany SSRI use. The drawback at this time is the need for twice-daily dosing and titrating the dose.
Norepinephrine-serotonin modulator, [specifically Mirtazapine (Remeron)]	A new antidepressant that appears to act in a manner similar to Venlafaxine[36,85]	Mirtazapine requires only a single daily dose, does not cause sexual dysfunction as a side effect, and has sedating properties that may be useful in treating depressed patients with marked insomnia.
Tricyclics and Tetracyclics	Increase availability of norepinephrine, serotonin, and dopamine in the synapse by blocking their reuptake	These medications are the standard treatments against which other newer medications were compared. Danger of toxicity in higher doses.
Monoamine Oxidase Inhibitors (MAOIs)	Inhibit the enzyme, monamine oxidase, in the central nervous system, intestinal track and platelets	

Medication Treatment Recommendations

Current recommendations about selecting an antidepressant indicate that clinicians should base decisions on:

- Anticipated side effects

- Safety or tolerability of these side effects for a given patient

- Patient preference

- Scientific evidence on the efficacy of the medication

- Cost

According to recent Practice Guidelines on depression it is suggested that the SSRIs, desimpramine, nortriptyline, buproprion, and venlafaxine are best suited for most patients.[36] Actually, the use of MAOIs should be restricted to patients who respond poorly to other treatments because of their potential for serious side effects.[36]

Because of the high rate (30-50 percent) of patient non-response to initial pharmacotherapy efforts, alternative medications should be tried for those patients who fail to respond to the initially prescribed medication.[86] For example, in comparisons of tricyclics and SSRIs used in sequence, between 30 and 50 percent of patients who did not respond to tricyclics did respond to an SSRI. In addition, a recent study found a positive response rate of 72 percent among patients who switched to sertraline (Zoloft) after failing to respond to fluoxetine (Prozac). These study results indicate that professionals should consider at least two trials of SSRI before switching to another medication

Relapse—The relapse rates for clients treated only with antidepressants are typically much higher than for clients who complete psychotherapy, especially cognitive-behavioral therapy.

Recent reviewers note that if patients discontinue taking antidepressant medications following recovery from depression, about 25 percent of those patients will relapse within the next two months.[36] These relapse rates have led many clinicians to recommend that antidepressants be taken for between four and six months, continuing even after depressive symptoms have remitted to reduce the risk of relapse.

The table on the following pages details the different types of medications, usual dosage, common side-effects, and any special concerns.[87]

Figure 5.2 Antidepressant Medications

Drug Name	Dose (mg/day)	Common Side-Effects	Special Concerns
Class: Selective Serotonin Reuptake Inhibitors (SSRI)			
Citalopram (Celexa)	20-60	**All SSRIs:** Sexual dysfunction, decreased appetite, nausea, fatigue, daytime sedation, nervousness, restlessness, and anxiety	**Special Concerns for all SSRIs:** • Because SSRI medications do not directly influence specific receptors or block the norepinephrine reuptake pump mechanism, they have a limited side effect and toxicity profile and are relatively safe in overdose.
Fluoxetine (Prozac)	20-80	Agitation, respiratory complaints, headache, dry mouth, tremors	• **Except for fluoxetine**, rapid discontinuation of SSRIs is commonly associated with symptoms of withdrawal, which persist for 1-2 weeks. Typical SSRI withdrawal symptoms include dizziness, headache, tingling, "electric-shock" sensations, and flu-like symptoms.
Fluvoxamine (Luvox)	50-300	Insomnia (especially if given in p.m.), agitation, confusion, headache, fine tremor, dizziness, diarrhea	• A single dose of the medication can be used to rapidly block withdrawal symptoms prior to reinstituting a more gradual tapering of the medication.
Paroxetine (Paxil)	10-80	Frequent urination, constipation, sweating, headache, fine tremor, dizziness, fatigue	• Allow at least 4-6 weeks before achieving a steady-state concentration when initiating treatment or modifying the dose.
Sertraline (Zoloft)	50-200	Nausea/diarrhea, dry mouth, insomnia, headache, fine tremor, dizziness	• Same client cautions as for tricyclic drugs. Chance of toxicity is less than with tricyclic drugs; symptoms include nausea, vomiting, tremor, irritability, and muscle spasms. • Use with other drugs may cause "serotonin syndrome" with nausea, diarrhea, chills, palpitations, agitation, muscle twitching, and delirium. • **Can be fatal if taken along with MAOI's.**
Class: Serotonin-Norepinephrine Reuptake Inhibitors			
Venlafaxine HCL (Effexor)	75-375	Nausea, headache, sedation, dry mouth, dizziness, insomnia, weight loss, sweating, diarrhea, weakness, nervousness, sexual disturbance (especially in males)	• Can produce elevations in blood pressure related to dose. • Although no studies yet, combination with MAOI is likely to produce serious, perhaps fatal, reaction.
Class: Dopamine-Norepinephrine Reuptake Inhibitors			
Bupropion (Wellbutrin)	150-450	Dry mouth, blurred vision, constipation, sweating, insomnia, headache, dizziness, hypertension, nausea/diarrhea	• Avoid use in patients with Anorexia or Bulimia due to seizure potential. • Can cause serotonergic syndrome with severe toxicity if combined with MAOI use.
Class: Selective-Noradrenaline Reuptake Inhibitors			
Reboxetine (Edronax, Vestra)	Pending FDA approval as of 02/01	Dry mouth, constipation increased sweating, insomnia, urinary hesitation retention, impotence, tachycardia, vertigo	• In clinical trails to date few serious adverse effects have been reported.
Class: Serotonin Modulators			
Nefazodone (Serzone)	150-300	Sedation, dizziness, nausea/dry mouth	• Can potentiate the effect of certain benzodiazepines. • Can cause serotonergic syndrome in combination with MAOI use.
Trazodone (Desyrel)	300-600	Sedation, dizziness, nausea/dry mouth	• Avoid use in patients with recent myocardial infarction. • May potentiate the effects of other sedating medications.

Continued on page 65

Antidepressant Medications Continued

Drug Name	Dose (mg/day)	Common Side-Effects	Special Concerns
Class: Norepinephrine-Serotonin Modulators			
Mirtazapine (Remeron)	15-45	Sedation which attenuates over time, dry mouth, weight gain, constipation, fatigue, dizziness, or the static hypertension	• Very rare occurrence of agranulocytosis, but does not require routine blood monitoring.
Class: Tricyclics			
Amitriptyline (Elavil)	75-300	Dry mouth, sedation, weight gain, blurred vision, constipation, sweating, disorientation, fine tremor dizziness heart palpitations, noninjurious ECG changes, and fatigue	*Special Concerns for All Tricyclics:* • With all cyclic drugs (mono-, tri-tetracyclics, di-benzoxapine, and triazolopyridine), therapeutic dose is close to toxic dose. Toxic symptoms are mostly anti-cholinergic (dry mouth, blurred vision, constipation, sweating, delayed urination).
Clomipramine (Anafranil)	75-250	Dry mouth, blurred vision, constipation, insomnia, fine tremor, dizziness, heart palpitations, noninjurious ECG changes, weight gain, sexual disturbance	• Next most common toxic symptoms are central nervous system effects (drowsiness, sedation, insomnia, excitement, disorientation/confusion, or headache).
Desipramine (Norpramin)	75-300	Dry mouth, heart palpitations	• Use in suicidal clients is risky.
Doxepin (Sinequan, Triadapin)	75-300	Dry mouth, sedation, blurred vision, constipation, dizziness, weight gain	• Tricyclics may lower seizure threshold; stopping abruptly can cause a syndrome with anxiety, fever, sweating, inflammation of the nasal mucosa, malaise, and other symptoms. Syndrome can also occur after large increases in dose.
Imipramine (Tofranil)	75-300	Dry mouth, dizziness, blurred vision, constipation, sweating, delayed urination in elderly, sedation, insomnia, headache, fine tremor heart palpitations, noninjurious changes in ECG, nausea/diarrhea, weight gain, sexual disturbance	• Stopping medication can result in rebound depression, although this appears to be minimized with gradual reduction in dose.
Nortriptyline (Aventyl, Pamelor)	50-200	Dry mouth, constipation, disorientation/confusion, fine tremor, fatigue	• Many interactions with other medications.
Protriptyline (Triptil, Vivactil)	15-60	Dry mouth, blurred vision, constipation, sweating, insomnia, dizziness noninjurious ECG changes, fatigue	
Trimipramine (Surmontil)	75-300	Sedation, dry mouth, constipation, confusion, fine tremor, dizziness, noninjurious ECG changes, weight gain	
Class: Tetracyclics			
Amoxapine (Asendin)	100-300	Dry mouth, constipation, delayed urination in elderly, sedation, insomnia, dizziness, heart palpitations, dermatitis/rash	• See concerns listed for Tricyclics. • Added risks of dopamine antagonist side effects such as tardive dyskinesia.
Maprotiline (Ludiomil)	75-200	Dry mouth, blurred vision, constipation, sedation, fine tremor, dermatitis, weight gain	• See concerns listed for Tricyclics. • Avoid use in patients with risk of alcohol or sedative withdrawal syndrome.

Continued on page 66

Antidepressant Medications Continued

Drug Name	Dose (mg/day)	Common Side-Effects	Special Concerns
Class: Monoamine Oxidase Inhibitors (MAOIs) Irreversible MAOIs			
Irreversible MAOIs Isocarboxazid (Marplan)	30-50	Dry mouth, headache, dizziness, nausea	**Special Concerns with MAOIs:** • Most important concern is that if clients consume foods rich in tyramine (e.g., aged cheese, meat extracts, sausage) or use over-the-counter drugs (e.g., cold remedies, anti-asthma drugs, and even vitamin supplements) can cause a high-blood pressure crisis indicated by headache, neck stiffness, nausea, vomiting, sweating (with fever or clammy skin), dilated pupils, photophobia, sudden nose bleed, chest pain, and rapid or slow heartbeat. • Overdoses can be fatal; changing to another antidepressant requires 10 days without medication. • Can produce withdrawal symptoms if stopped suddenly. • **Can be fatal if taken along with SSRIs.**
Phenelzine (Nardil)	45-90	Dry mouth, blurred vision, constipation, sedation, insomnia, fine tremor, dizziness, heart palpitations, nausea, weight gain, sexual disturbance	
Tranylcypromine (Parnate)	20-60	Dry mouth, sedation, insomnia, dizziness, heart palpitations	
Reversible MAOIs Moclobemide (Manerix)	300-600	Dry mouth, insomnia, headache, dizziness	

In the case of individuals suffering from two or more depressive episodes, clinicians may recommend that clients remain on the medication for the rest of their lives to prevent relapse.

Possible explanations for the high relapse rates following medication treatment include:[19]

- Fewer than 10 percent of those suffering from Major Depression are likely to receive a therapeutic dose of their medication.

- More than 20 percent of patients fail to follow through and fill prescribed antidepressant medication.

- Most patients who do begin treatment tend to stop taking the medicine too soon (within 14 weeks).

These factors point to the vital importance of educating depression sufferers about the risk of depressive recurrence and steps they can take to reduce the possibility of relapse.

Research indicates that relapse can be reduced by continuing to take medications for a period of time following symptom improvement. Similarly, patients who responded to cognitive behavior therapy during the acute phase of depression and were then offered continuation phase therapy for the next two years had significantly lower relapse rates than those who discontinued therapy.[19,36] Therefore, cognitive behavior therapy may also be an effective continuation therapy following treatment with antidepressants.[36]

How Effective are Psychotropic Medications for Treating Depression?

Substantial research supports the efficacy of using psychotropic medications to treat clinical depression.[88,89] However, there is no one predominant medication recommended or found effective for treating clinical depression. Often a combination of medications proves effective, particularly a tricyclic and neuroleptic combination for psychotic depression. Researchers have found MAOIs effective for treating atypical depression, while tricyclic medications tend to relieve melancholic features including weight loss, middle and late insomnia, and psychomotor disturbance.[83,90]

What is the Effectiveness of Using Medications Versus Psychotherapy?

Echoing the earlier discussion about whether depression is caused by a "chemical imbalance" or is the result of psychological processes, treatment outcome researchers most often compare psychotherapy and medication.

There is ample evidence that psychotherapy is at least as effective, and in some ways more effective, than using medications to treat depression.[91] Many meta-analyses of treatment outcomes have found that psychotherapy has an effect approximately twice as great as that for medications.[92-94] While acknowledging that the debate between medication and therapy is a "hotly debated topic," some reviewers assert that pharmacotherapy is the care standard for those experiencing psychotic depression and for depressed inpatients.[86] They point out that given today's shortened lengths of stay for depressed inpatients, psychotherapy is not usually a viable treatment option. Psychotherapy should also be reserved for patients who refuse pharmacotherapy.

One area of controversy involves whether or not psychotherapy is more effective when combined with medications than alone. A review of 17 controlled outcome studies found that combined treatment was only marginally better than therapy or medication alone.[95] Another meta-analysis concluded that cognitive therapy was as effective as medication in the treatment of the *acute depressive episode*. This research found that combined treatment did not appear superior to either treatment conducted alone.[65] On the other hand, some

*acute depressive episode—
rapid onset, relatively short
time being depressed*

67

researchers have compared interpersonal therapy (IPT) and medication and found that IPT therapy was better for relieving adjustment problems such as mood, apathy, suicidal ideation, and loss of pleasure. These comparisons found medications better for relieving sleep, appetite, and concentration problems. They concluded that combined treatments were superior to medication or psychotherapy alone.[55] These results suggest that the type of therapy practiced may determine whether or not combined medication and therapy are superior to either mode used exclusively.

Recent treatment guidelines have suggested that combined modalities be considered as a first-line intervention for mild or moderate-to-severe depression if the following scenarios exist.

- *For Mild Depression*: Use a combined approach when the patient prefers, there is a history of partial response to a single modality, or there is a history of poor compliance with medication.

- *For Moderate-to-Severe Depression*: Use a combined approach in cases involving prominent psychosocial issues, interpersonal problems, personality disorder, or a poor medication compliance history.

One area in which psychotherapy appears to outperform medication is in producing lower relapse rates. Based on the results of one- to two-year follow-up studies, researchers concluded that the overall relapse rate for cognitive therapy clients was 30 percent, compared with 60 percent for the medication group.[96] Also, an 18-month follow-up of the NIMH collaborative study concluded that the effectiveness of cognitive therapy was insignificant when compared to other forms of treatment, but was ranked the best on 11 of 13 outcome measures.[51,97] They also concluded that those treated with cognitive therapy had the highest recovery rate and the highest percentage of recovery without relapse.

In summary, clients who were treated exclusively with antidepressant medication:[51]

- Sought help more during the follow-up period

- Had more incidences of relapse

- Experienced fewer weeks of minimal or no symptoms compared to those who were treated exclusively with cognitive therapy

Medication appeared to elevate mood and relieve depression faster in some clients, but by the end of the treatment period, psychotherapy produced the same or a greater level of improvement.[51] The reviews of relapse rates given above demonstrate that while medications may produce short-term relief for depressed clients, psychotherapy seems to offer more long-term effectiveness. However, using medications for longer periods of time equalizes the effectiveness. For example, clients treated with medications for three months had relapse rates twice as high as those who completed cognitive therapy, while clients treated for 15 months had the same relapse rates as for cognitive therapy.[98] Furthermore, some authors caution against long-term use of medication treatment, citing evidence that suggests that although maintenance pharmacotherapy may suppress relapse, it does so by slowing or negatively impacting the natural recovery of the central nervous system.[99]

Another important finding from these studies reveals that there is no difference between treatment effectiveness with regard to the severity of depression.[51,100-102] This discovery challenges the frequent claim that psychotherapy, particularly cognitive therapy, does not work as well with severely depressed individuals.

Medications, at least in the short-term, can be more cost-effective than psychotherapy, principally because clients and physicians compare the cost of a dose of antidepressant medication to the cost of a session of psychotherapy. However, this cost comparison ignores the evidence showing higher relapse rates for medications than psychotherapy, perhaps creating the necessity for lifelong medication treatment in order to prevent relapse. Psychotherapy and medication treatment may be at least equivalent in cost in the long-run, and psychotherapy may be more cost-effective over a lifetime.

In addition, reviewers have noted that nonmedical psychotherapists may wait far too long to refer a patient for pharmacotherapy.[86] Conversely, these reviewers found that a significant percentage of chronically depressed patients unresponsive to pharmacotherapy appear to benefit from symptom-focused psychotherapy.

Thase and Kupfer may offer the best overall conclusion to this debate:[86] "Rather than dissipate our professional energies in turf battles over whose treatments are better for patients with inherently good prognoses…collaboration aimed at maximizing delivery of effective treatment to larger numbers of depressed people should receive highest priority. Such collaborative efforts, coupled with continued public education, represent the best hope for our patients and their families, now and in the future."

What is Electro-Convulsive Therapy (ECT)?

In line with suggested treatment guidelines, clinicians should consider ECT when dealing with those who manifest with chronic or moderate-to-severe levels of depression.[36] ECT should also be considered in cases in which psychotic symptoms or *catatonia* are evident or in cases where the patient expresses preference for this treatment and/or has benefitted from it in the past. Patients who may express suicidal ideation and refuse to eat should also be considered for ECT.

catatonia—extreme muscle rigidity. A person in a catatonic state may remain in a fixed position for long periods of time.

ECT induces a seizure through an external electrical source. It has a bad reputation as being a barbaric treatment for mental illness or depression, a reputation that is not fully deserved. At least 75 percent of clients with severe depression improve following ECT.[9] The exact mechanism by which ECT improves depression is unknown, but it is known that almost all neurotransmitters implicated in mental illness are effected by the procedure. The total number of treatments required for a full therapeutic effect ranges from 6 to 20. If there is no effect after 12 to 15 treatments, ECT probably can't help alleviate the person's depression.[87]

ECT's use in movies like One Flew Over the Cuckoo's Nest was portrayed as severely negative and used as a method to control the patients rather than to treat them.

Recent reviewers concluded that:[36]

- ECT has the highest response rate of ANY form of antidepressant treatment (80-90 percent of patients show improvement).

- ECT should routinely be considered for most cases of moderate-to-severe depression where the patient has been nonresponsive to other treatment modalities.

- Even patients who are medication resistant tend to show a 50 percent chance of improvement using ECT.

- ECT may be the treatment of choice for individuals suffering from psychotic depression, especially if they have not responded to pharmacotherapy.

- ECT should be considered for those who suffer catatonic depression, present severe suicidality, refuse to eat, are pregnant, or desire a rapid antidepressant response.[36]

ECT has been considered generally to be safer than many forms of combined antidepressant treatments. In general, risks do not exceed those associated with anesthesia. However, ECT could result in cardiovascular and neurological side effects; therefore, its use in patients with significant cardiovascular disease or increased intracranial pressure should be cautiously evaluated.[36]

At one extreme, ECT side-effects can include death, usually due to cardiac arrest. However, ECT might only cause death in .01 to .08 percent of those receiving treatment, while estimates of those diagnosed with depression who would have died (usually through suicide) without treatment are about 10 percent.[83] The other major side effect is memory loss, particularly for what occurred during the days immediately preceding treatment. An immediate period of confusion and disorientation follows treatment, but this usually clears up in a short time.

Another downside to ECT is the relapse rate. While ECT appears to provide acute relief in life-threatening types of situations, there is no evidence that it provides long-term benefits or that it prevents future relapse into depression. One study notes that about half of clients who receive ECT relapse within one year. If these clients are treated with follow-up antidepressant medications, the relapse rate drops to about 20 percent.[83] These results clearly illustrate the importance of careful follow-up to prevent future episodes of depression.

Thus, evidence exists that correct use of ECT can be especially effective for those suffering from depression with intense suicidal or psychotic features.[103-106] One study noted that ECT was not nearly as effective for clients suffering from depression caused by stress or situational factors.[107]

Possible ECT Side Effects

- *Memory loss for some events in the days preceding the ECT*
- *Patchy memory loss for events following ECT with no evidence of permanent memory loss*
- *Rapid heart beat and high blood pressure may be pronounced for several minutes following treatment*
- *Spontaneous seizures at about the same proportion as that found in the general population*
- *Headache and muscle pain that is not usually severe*[83]

What Other Biological Treatments Exist?

Other biologically based treatments include the use of St John's Wort (an herb), exercise, and phototherapy (a type of bright light therapy).

St. John's Wort

This herb has garnered wide attention for its purported antidepressant effects; however, since it is not a regulated drug, many of the preparations available to patients are non-standardized, making it difficult to know the preparation potency or to regulate the dose. Recent studies indicate that for patients with mild-to-moderate depression, St. John's Wort was more effective than placebo, was generally comparable in effectiveness to low doses of tricyclic medications, and resulted in less side effects than tricyclic medications.[36]Investigators also indicate that combined use of St. John's Wort with MAOIs is contraindicated, and the fact that the herb provides an antidepressant effect should argue for caution in any double use of St. John's Wort with a prescribed antidepressant. Patients considering this double use should discuss this approach with the prescribing professional.

Exercise

A recent review of exercise as a treatment intervention for various conditions noted that aerobic exercise can be more effective than placebo and no-treatment conditions for mild-to-moderate depression.[99] These authors also note studies that have found the effectiveness of exercise to be comparable to individual, group, and cognitive psychotherapy. Indeed, exercise may function as a pleasant event in its own right. Significant benefit can be achieved after approximately five weeks with supervised exercise sessions occurring at least three times per week. These sessions should consist of aerobic or nonaerobic activity of low-to-moderate intensity, lasting from 20-60 minutes each. Researchers also noted that maintaining treatment gains depends on continuing activity for at least a year. Another advantage is that exercise is significantly more cost effective than other forms of depression treatment.

Phototherapy

Early trials in the 1980s suggested bright light therapy to alleviate depression; however these were challenged until recent controlled studies provided preliminary support for using Phototherapy to reduce depression that has a seasonal component (particularly the winter "blues"). Research also supports Phototherapy as a form of adjunctive therapy for those with chronic Major Depression or Dysthymia with seasonal exacerbations.[36] Reported improvement rates have been as high as 40-50 percent for persons suffering from winter depression after one week of treatment, but there is also evidence that relapse may occur if light therapy is withdrawn.[86] Side effects are fairly rare, but can include headache, eye strain, irritability, insomnia, and occasionally hypomania. Treatment guidelines suggest that combined antidepressant and light therapy may:[36]

- Increase the effectiveness of both treatment forms

- Should be considered in cases where neither therapy can be used at full dosages.

Patients receiving both treatments should be advised that some antidepressants can result in sensitivity to light exposure.

Therapy Notes
From the Desk of
Pat Owen

Terminated with C.R. today following 6 months of individual and pharmacological therapy. Much improved functioning. C. was able to maintain job and is currently being considered for a promotion.

C. responded well to CBT with the focus on reducing the inertia, changing irrational cognitions related to perfectionism, guilt, death of mother, taking care of father, and unresolved feelings with deceased mother. Referring C. for marital therapy with spouse to focus on interpersonal interactions that reinforce C's depressive symptoms. Affect is normal, no suicidal ideation. Sleep is normal, moderate use of alcohol (3-4 oz./week), increased activities with participation again in kids' after school activities, exercising (took up tennis). Reinforced relapse prevention with continued use of cognitive and behavioral strategies, given history of depression and possibility for future episode. C. cracked a joke and laughed on the way out, after thanking me and saying, "I hope to never see you again."

Appendix: Depression Assessment Instruments

Client-Rated Self Report Instruments

Zung Scale and Center for Epidemiological Studies Depression Scale (CES-D) [108,109]— These inventories are easy to administer and contain fewer than 30 items that require 15-30 minutes for adults to complete. Each instrument produces a global score that is the sum of the weighted item ratings. Weighted item ratings relate to severity of a symptom. Researchers interpret that score on a range from normal to depressed.

The CES-D is an instrument that has been most widely used in identifying cases for research in community studies of depression. Some research suggests that the results of the Zung scale may be significantly closer to structured diagnostic interview results than the CES-D. In addition, recent studies indicate that the CES-D tends to create many false positives, indicating persons are depressed when in fact they are not.[110] Such findings have lead some authors to suggest not using the CES-D as a clinical diagnostic instrument, although it may still have utility for case finding in research.[111] The Zung scale covers five of the DSM diagnostic criteria for depression with four other criteria partially covered.

Beck's Depression Inventory-II (BDI-2)[112]— The BDI assesses depressive symptoms based on the DSM-IV criteria. The client is asked to respond to 21 items covering specific thoughts and feelings in the areas of cognitive, affective, somatic, and vegetative symptoms of depression they have experienced within the past week. It is useful for those 13 years and older and can be administered individually, in groups, in a written format, or oral format. It takes approximately 5-10 minutes to complete. It can be scored manually or by computer, and a computer-based interpretation is available. It is intended to be a screening tool for depression, with particular attention to items on hopelessness and suicidal ideation as the best indicators of potential suicidality.[113,114]

Beck Cognition Checklist— This instrument assesses automatic thoughts related to anxiety and depression and has two subscales:

1. The CCL-A, which measures anxiety symptoms

2. The CCL-D, which assesses depressive cognitions

A recent study evaluated the utility of the CCL with psychiatric outpatients and college students.[115] For the CCL-D, validity results were positive, and the subscale differentiated students from outpatients and outpatients by diagnostic groups. In another application of the instrument, medically ill patients were compared with psychiatric inpatients and controls.[116] The authors found that depressed psychiatric inpatients showed negative cognitive patterns when compared with depressed medically ill patients, who were best distinguished by symptoms of anhedonia, low amounts of positive affect, and physiological hyperarousal.

Geriatric Depression Scale (GDS)[117]— The GDS was developed to discriminate depressive symptoms from general characteristics of aging in the elderly population. It can be used as a self-report instrument or in an interview format. It has 30 items in a yes/no format that indicate depression. A short form of the GDS, developed from the items with the highest correlation to depression, has 15 items that require an average of 5-7 minutes to complete.

A recent review of assessment instruments for the elderly concluded that the Geriatric Depression Scale (GDS) was the best-validated instrument for geriatric populations.[118] However, other reviewers noted that, in severely demented individuals, there was no well-validated scale; thus with this population, the GDS was considered unreliable. Instead, they recommended the Cornell Scale for Depression in Dementia (CSDD), for individuals with both dementia and possible depression.[119] *See the Structured Interview section for more information on CSDD.*

General Issues Related to Self-Report Measures

One concern with self-report measures is that the instruments are typically "*face valid.*" This concern is not serious in outpatient treatment settings, where therapists also use other instruments to screen for depression, conduct follow-up interviews, and utilize other clinical evidence for diagnosis. However, in research settings, clients could exaggerate the degree of distress they report. Coyne and others contend that most empirical depression studies using self-report instruments are, in fact, measuring self-reported general distress rather than clinical depression.[120,121] Especially, in forensic settings, therapists should always cross-check self-report data with other evidence.

Structured Interview and Clinician Rated Systems

Hamilton Rating Scale for Depression (HRSD)[122]— Historically, the HRSD is the most common interview method for assessing depression. It was initially created to assess depression severity in those already diagnosed and has become a common outcome measure for evaluating the effects of different treatment interventions, especially drug therapies and inpatient treatments.[111] The HRSD is a 21-item scale completed during a 30-minute interview. It is reliable and shows moderately good relationships to other measures of depression, as well as being sensitive to changes in symptoms over time. In addition, the HRSD has been modified to extend its usefulness based on continued use. For instance, both a computerized version and a paper-and-pencil self-report version have been developed.[123,124]

A recent study in a primary care setting compared the HRSD with the Beck Depression Inventory, concluded that they were related to one another and showed similar rates of improvement over the course of treatment. However, the authors noted that since the two scales emphasized different dimensions of depression, they would be more useful when used together.[125]

The Structured Clinical Interview for DSM-IV Axis I Disorders (SCID)[126] — The SCID is designed for use by trained interviewers to ensure a structured and consistent format for investigating psychiatric symptoms. Both the research version (SCID-RV) and the clinical version (SCID-CV) yield results based on DSM-IV diagnoses. They rate the severity of depressive symptoms based on the number of symptoms present and the interviewer's estimate of the degree of impairment.

The SCID-CV clinical version takes about 30-60 minutes to complete and examines only disorders that are frequently seen in clinical settings. The full research version (SCID-RV) takes 1.5 to 2 hours to complete and measures 32 different diagnoses, including major mental health and substance use disorders. The instrument demonstrates adequate reliability and validity for diagnostic purposes.

Schedule for Affective Disorders and Schizophrenia (SADS)[127] — The SADS uses a structured and consistent format for investigating psychiatric symptoms. The SADS, interviewers should be "highly trained individuals with extensive clinical knowledge."[111] The SADS is designed to evaluate current and lifetime affective disorders and yields diagnoses consistent with research criteria for studying depression, including other diagnostic categories. The instrument is a semistructured interview divided into two parts and takes approximately 1.5 to 2 hours to administer. It covers symptoms of major psychiatric disorders, including depression. Part I obtains a detailed description of the clinical features of the current episode and during the week prior to the interview. Part II obtains historical information needed to confirm a lifetime diagnosis. It is also provides estimates of severity. The questions are progressive and have built in criteria for whether to rule-in or rule-out the symptom for current diagnostic purposes. The SADS was found to be more effective than the DIS in diagnosing depressive disorders.[128] However, the SADS has not been updated for DSM-IV diagnostic criteria.

The Diagnostic Interview Schedule (DIS-IV)[129] *and the Computerized Diagnostic Interview (C-DIS)*[130] — The DIS is a structured diagnostic interview designed to be administered by experienced lay interviewers without clinical training. The computerized version can be self-administered with availability of an assistant to answer questions if needed. The DIS has been used in psychiatric survey research for decades to assess the pre-valence of psychiatric disorders in the general population. Modules included in the DIS are Mood, Anxiety, Schizophrenia, Eating, Somatization, Psychoactive Substance Abuse, and Antisocial Personality Disorders. The DIS provides both current and lifetime diagnostic information.

The Composite International Diagnostic Interview (CIDI)[131,132] — Similar to the DIS, the CIDI is a structured diagnostic interview for all DSM-IV diagnoses designed for survey research employing lay rather than clinician interviewers. It is most frequently used for research rather than for diagnosis when identifying depression cases for further study. The SCID or the HRSD would better serve clinical diagnostic needs than the CIDI.

Cornell Scale for Depression in Dementia (CSDD)[119] — An interviewer-administered scale using combined information from both the patient and an outside informant (such as a family member). The Cornell Scale measures factors such as: depression, biological rhythm disruption, agitation/psychosis, and negative symptoms (e.g., anhedonia and poor concentration).

Combined Instruments

Primary Care Evaluation of Mental Disorders (PRIME-MD) — This instrument recently received increased research attention and was developed primarily for use in primary care settings by physicians.[133] The PRIME-MD consists of a questionnaire completed by the patient prior to seeing the physician. The physician then follows-up with additional questions in a clinical interview. Two questions on the PRIME-MD are specific to depression: one dealing with anhedonia (loss of pleasure) and another dealing with depressed mood. Responses to these two questions were found to accurately classify 96 percent of depressed patients in this setting.

Accurately identifying non-depressed patients can also be achieved with this instrument as well. If, for example, the patient endorses either of the screening items (anhedonia or depressed mood), then the physician asks additional questions about four core areas of functioning — sleep disturbance, appetite change, anhedonia, and low self-esteem. Patients reporting at least two of the above four symptoms correctly identified almost all depressed patients (97 percent) and also correctly identified non-depressed patients (94 percent).[134]

Recently, the PRIME-MD was converted to a patient-only questionnaire, which was found to be more efficient in terms of the physician's time and about as accurate as the PRIME-MD when used as a self-report instrument along with physician interviews.[135]

Harvard Department of Psychiatry/ National Depression Screening Day Scale (HANDS)[136] — In recent years, the National Depression Screening Day (NDSD) has been inaugurated across the country to encourage people to:

- Become informed about depression
- Take a brief inventory to assess for depression (typically the Zung inventory)
- Have assessment information reviewed by a mental health professional and receive feedback

Hoping to improve the efficiency of the screening day, investigators at Harvard created the Harvard Department of Psychiatry/NDSD scale (HANDS). All diagnoses were confirmed with the Structured Clinical Interview for DSM-IV Axis I Disorders (SCID). The final HANDS had only 10 items, but was reported to have performed as well as the 20-item Zung, the 21-item BDI-II, and the 15-item Hopkins Symptom Depression Checklist. Additionally, HANDS was designed for general applicability in clinical settings apart from NDSD.

Suicide Assessment Scales

Beck Hopelessness Scale (BHS) — The BHS measures negative attitudes about the future (pessimism), and is helpful in evaluating suicide potential. It makes a good complimentary assessment tool to other measures of depression. The BHS is a 20 item self-report instrument useful for adults age 17 and older. It takes approximately 5-10 minutes to complete with computer scoring and interpretation available. It outperforms the BDI in accounting for suicide risk. Scores of 9 or more predict eventual suicide (within 5-10 years) for those who are depressed and have suicidal ideation. The ability of this instrument to assess suicide risk highlights the link between hopelessness and depression.[114,137]

Beck Scale for Suicidal Ideation — This scale detects and measures the severity of suicidal ideation in adults and adolescents. It is a 21 item scale that can be administered to adults age 17 and older, individually or in groups, and takes approximately 5-10 minutes to complete. It has computer scoring and interpretation available. This tool is especially useful in settings where clinical evaluation for suicide is not available or for clinicians not fully trained in recognizing suicidal tendencies. The instrument has good validity and reliability and is best used for monitoring quality and quantity of changes of ongoing suicidal ideation.[114,138,139]

Firestone Assessment of Self-destructive Thoughts — This instrument was designed to assist in clinical assessment of suicide potential for adults age 16 and over. It is developed to be administered in a group setting and takes approximately 20 minutes to complete. It measures 11 levels of progressively self-destructive thoughts on a continuum that includes Social Isolation, Eating Disorders, Substance Abuse, Self-Mutilation, and Suicide.[114]

Suicide Probability Scale (SPS) — This self-report scale measure attitudes and behaviors relevant to suicide risk for people age 14 and older. This 36 item scale takes approximately 5-10 minutes to complete and can be administered individually or in groups. It yields scores on five scales; Hopelessness, Suicide Ideation, Negative Self-Evaluations, Hostility, and a Total Score. The test is based on concepts related to suicide potential but does not assess known risk factors.[114,140]

Psychometric Assessments

In both inpatient and outpatient settings, clinicians regularly use psychometric instruments to facilitate diagnosis and describe client personality characteristics.

Rorschach Inkblot Test — The Rorschach consists of ten cards with randomly created inkblots, some in monochrome and some in color. The cards are shown to clients one at a time, and their answers are recorded and later scored. This test is a "projective" measure of personality, revealing information that can be very useful in diagnosis and treatment planning.

There are many systems available for scoring and interpreting responses to the Rorschach test. The most widely used is the Exner Method, which defines a comprehensive system for administering, scoring, and interpreting Rorschach results.[141] Many consider this to be the best system to use for two reasons:

1. Its large normative base allows the clinician to determine how unusual a particular score is for a particular client.

2. This system has survived a great deal of research on its validity and utility. Helpful indices are made up of combined test scores and help diagnose depression successfully. For example, Exner's Depression Index (DEPI) utilizes seven key indicators drawn from the Rorschach's results. Exner indicates that individuals who score a 5 on the index share many features with those who are diagnosed as depressed, but the actual diagnosis may vary depending on history and presentation. Scores of 6 out of 7 indicate a serious affective problem.

Equating a high score on the DEPI with a diagnosis of Major Depression can be problematic because schizophrenics may often score in this range. When this occurs, these scores usually indicate that the schizophrenic person is also depressed. The score taken by itself cannot be directly equated with a Major Depressive Episode.[141]

Because the Rorschach is both time-intensive and labor-intensive, it is an inefficient tool for diagnosis. However, this test produces information especially useful for developing treatment plans and understanding a client's therapy progress.

MMPI and MMPI-2 — These instruments are widely used to assess individuals who present depressive symptoms. The original MMPI consists of 566 statements about the person taking the test (e.g., "I wake up fresh and refreshed most mornings," "It is safer to trust nobody."). Clients are asked to rate whether these items are true or false. The test is then scored, often electronically, and a profile constructed indicating test-taking attitude, clinical problems, and content analysis of specific scales.[142] The test was revised and is now called the MMPI-2.[143]

Both versions of the MMPI have a "scale 2" originally developed to assess symptoms and features of clinical depression, including denial of happiness and self-worth, physical and somatic complaints associated with depression, and lack of interest in the environment. According to Graham, this scale is a valuable indicator of the client's discomfort and dissatisfaction with life. He suggests that very elevated scores (T-scores above 80) indicate clinical depression, and clients with scores in this range often receive depressive diagnoses. More moderate scores (probably T-scores in the 60s) tend to indicate a lifestyle characterized by poor morale and lack of involvement.[144] Moderate scores on this scale have also been found in individuals who recently underwent a major life change or transition such as hospitalization or incarceration. As with the Rorschach test, scores on this scale are not specific enough for diagnosis; clinicians must consider other information when evaluating the results.

Thematic Apperception Test (TAT) — The TAT, like the Rorschach, is a projective test which presents clients with a series of ambiguous black and white pictures. Clients are asked to make up a story about the picture. The theory behind the TAT is that clients will project into their stories the prominent themes and conflicts in their own lives. However, there is no normative base to use when comparing client responses. Despite this, many clinicians continue to use the test, scoring it according to the rules developed for the theoretical system with which they are familiar. The TAT is not in itself an efficient tool for diagnosing depression. However, information gained from the TAT may help clinicians develop treatment plans and understand the complexity of the client's life.

Glossary

A

acute depressive episode—*rapid onset of depression and short duration of episode*

anaclitic depression—*depressive feelings of abandonment based on the real or perceived loss of one's significant caretaker from childhood*

anhedonia—*marked lack of interest in pleasurable activities*

arbitrary inference—*jumping to conclusions*

atypical depression—*mood brightens at times, excessive sleeping, heavy feeling in arms and legs*

C

catatonia—*extreme muscle regidity. A person in a catatonic state may remain in a fixed position for long periods of time.*

catecholamine—*a group of neurotransmitters*

catharsis—*tension release following the expression of long repressed emotion allowing the client to experience, in the safety of the clinician's office, the emotion that could not be expressed as a child*

caudate area—*basal ganglia area of the brain involved in voluntary control move*

chronic—*episode has lasted at least two years*

circumstantiality—*manner of talking that is extremely indirect and "circular"*

cognitions—*thoughts*

comorbid—*the simultaneous presence of two or more disorders*

constricted affect—*the client appears apathetic and does not display much emotion*

D

delusions—*beliefs firmly held despite contradicting evidence*

dementia—*loss of intellectual capacity in such areas as memory, judgement, reasoning usually due to brain deterioration*

dichotomous (black/white) thinking—*thinking in extremes such as allowance, idealization of others or devaluation of others, never or always*

double depression—*intense Major Depressive Episode is superimposed upon the milder, chronic depressive disorder called Dysthymia*

dysthymia—*a persistent, low-level Depression that has been ongoing for two years*

E

epidemiological study—*research to estimate the prevalence of a disorder in the community (in this case depression)*

F

face valid—*the person taking the test can tell what the test is measuring by the wording of the test items*

H

hallucinations—*sensory perceptions without external stimulation; hearing voices or seeing things others do not see*

hippocampus—*large, complex, sea-horse shaped brain structure, involved in emotion, motivation, learning and long term memory functioning*

homework—*exercises conducted by the client outside of the therapy session*

I

IQ—*Intelligence Quotient, a measure of intelligence scores between 90 and 110 are considered "average"*

in vivo exposure—*conducting therapy in the environment that represents the client's most feared situation*

indoleamine—*a group of neurotransmitters that effect the central nervous system*

interpreting—*the therapist reflects to the client a clinical hypothesis regarding the connection between unconscious material and current or conscious material*

introjective depression—*anger turned inward; anger toward ones' external parents that couldn't be expressed for fear of rejection and thus results in punitive reactions towards ones' self*

L

labile affect—*emotions that change and vary widely*

learned helplessness—*learned expectations that one's efforts will have no effect on outcome*

M

magnification/minimization—*magnifying negative and minimizing positive interpretations of events*

mania—*unwarranted euphoria, grandiosity, pressured speech, decreased need for sleep, disturbances of thought processes such as circumstantiality, and impulsive behavior that often results in negative consequences, (e.g., one-night stands, gambling, speeding, drug use).*

melancholic—*worse depression in a.m., early morning awakening*

meta-analysis—*a statistical analysis of multiple studies with an assessment of overall treatment effects*

middle insomnia—*waking in the middle of the night with difficulty getting back to sleep*

mixed episode—*the person presenting with depression also manifests current or past symptoms of mania*

monoamine oxidase—*one of the enzymes present in the presynaptic terminal which breaks down catecholamines and idoleamines*

monoamine oxidase inhibitor (MAOI)—*a medication (iproniazid) originally created to treat Tuberculosis that has been noted to improve depression as well*

mood congruent psychotic symptoms—*the content of the delusion or hallucination matches depressive symptoms (e.g. "I am dead.")*

mood incongruent—*the content of the delusion (or hallucination) does not match the Depression*

N

neurotransmitters—*chemical agents in the brain that effect behavior, mood, and feelings*

norepinephrine—*type of catecholamine that effects the central nervous system functioning*

O

object relations—*"objects" are the internal representation of "others" who are the focus of love or affection. Thus, object relations are the present or past relationships with these internalized love objects.*

overgeneralization—*drawing a general conclusion from a specific incident*

P

personalization—*assuming outside events are related to oneself without evidence*

positive reinforcement—*an event following a person's behavior that increases the frequency of that behavior*

postpartum—*Depression occurs within four weeks of having a baby*

projective measure of personality—*stimuli that are assumed to be neutral are presented to the client. Thus, shapes, movement, descriptions, and other elements that clients' report are a product of their own experiences and perceptual orientation.*

psychotic—*impairment in awareness of reality, including symptoms of delusions and/or hallucinations*

psychotropic medications—*medications that effect behavior, emotions and/or cognitive processes*

R

reinforcement—*any event that increases the frequency of the preceding behavior*

rumination—*thinking the same thoughts repeatedly*

S

schemata—*belief systems through which events are interpreted*

selective abstraction—*only attending to one detail in a series of events or stimuli*

serotonin—*a neurotransmitter from the indoleamine group, which effects central nervous system functioning*

symbiotic—*self and other are perceived as the same (e.g., child sees mother as an extension of self)*

T

T-Scores—*standardized scores based on a scale of 1 to 100 with 50 as the mean*

terminal insomnia—*waking hours earlier than usual with no getting back to sleep*

transference—*the displacing of emotions or attitudes from the client onto the therapist based on past experiences*

tricyclic medications—*class of antidepressant medications effecting three neurotransmitters*

Bibliography

1. Gilbert, P. (1984). <u>Depression: From psychology to brain state.</u> Hillsdale, NJ: Lawrence Erlbaum Associates, Ltd.

2. Seligman, M.E. (1975). <u>Helplessness: On Depression, development and death</u>. San Francisco: Freeman.

3. American Psychiatric Association (1994). <u>Diagnostic and statistical manual of mental disorders</u> (4th ed.). Washington, DC: American Psychiatric Association.

4. Regier, D.A., Farmer, M.E., Rae, D.S., Myers, J.K., et. al. (1993). One-month prevalence of mental disorders in the United States and sociodemographic characteristics: The epidemiologic catchment area study. <u>Acta Psychiatric Scandia</u>, <u>88</u>: 35-47,

5. Regier, .D.A. & Robins, L. (1991). Introduction. In L. Robins & E. Regier (Eds). <u>Psychiatric Disorders in America</u>. New York: Free Press.

6. Kessler, R.C., Nelson, C.B., McGonagle, K.A., Liu, J., Swartz, M. & Blazer, D.G. (1996). Comorbidity of DSM-III-R major depressive disorder in the general population: Results from the U.S. National Comorbidity Survey. <u>British Journal of Psychiatry</u>,

7. Kaelber, C.T., Moul, D.E. & Farmer, M.E. (1995). Epidemiology of Depression. In E.E. Beckham & W.R. Leber (Eds). <u>Handbook of Depression (2nd Ed)</u>. New York: Guilford Press.

8. Nolen-Hoeksema, S. (1987). Sex differences in depression: Theory and evidence. <u>Psychological Bulletin</u>, <u>101</u>, 259-282.

9. Seligman, M.E. (1993). <u>What you can change & what you can't: the complete guide to successful self-improvement.</u> New York: Alfred A. Knopf.

10. Nolen-Hoeksema, S. (1990). <u>Sex differences in Depression</u>. Stanford, CA: Stanford University Press.

11. Weiss, J., Simson, P., Ambrose, M., Webster, A., & Hoffman, L. (1985). Neurochemical basis of behavioral depression. <u>Advances in Behavioral Medicine I</u>, 253-275.

12. Kuhl, J. (1981). Motivational and functional helplessness: The moderating effect of state- versus action-orientation. <u>Journal of Personality and Social Psychology</u>, <u>40</u>, 155-170.

13. McCarthy, M. (1990). The thin ideal, Depression, and eating disorders in women. <u>Behavior Research and Therapy</u>, <u>28</u>, 205-215.

14. Girgus, J., Nolen-Hoeksema, S., Seligman, M., Paul, G., & Spears, H. (1991). <u>Why do girls become more depressed than boys in early adolescence?</u> Paper presented at the meeting of the American Psychological Association, San Francisco.

15. Robins, L., Helzer, J., Weissman, M., Orvaschel, H., Gruenberg, E., Burke, J., & Regier, J. (1984). Lifetime prevalence of specific psychiatric disorders in three sites. <u>Archives of General Psychiatry</u>, <u>41</u>, 949-958.

16. Klerman, G. & Weissman, M. (1989). Increasing rates of Depression. <u>Journal of the American Medical Association</u>, <u>261</u>, 2229-2235.

17. Klerman, G., Lavori, P., Rice, J., Reich, T., Endicott, J., Andreason, N., Keller, M., & Hirschfeld, R. (1985). Birth-cohort trends in rates of Major Depressive Disorder among relatives of patients with Affective Disorder. <u>Archives of General Psychiatry</u>, <u>42</u>, 689-693.

18. Melfi, C.A., Chawla, A.J., Croghan, T.W., Hanna, M.P., Kennedy, S., & Sredl, K. (1998). The effects of adherence to antidepressant treatment guidelines on relapse and recurrence of depression. <u>Archives of General Psychiatry</u>, <u>55</u>, 1128-1132.

19. Keller, M.B. & Boland, R.J. (1998). Implications of failing to achieve successful long-term maintenance treatment of recurrent unipolar major depression. <u>Biological Psychiatry</u>, <u>44</u>, 348-360.

20. Van Gastel, A., Schotte, C., & Maes, M. (1997). The prediction of suicidal intent in depressed patients. Acta Psychiatrica Scandinavica, 96, 254-259.

21. Beckham, E.E., Leber, W.R., & Youll, L.K. (1995). The diagnostic classification of depression. In E.E. Beckham & W.R. Leber (Eds). Handbook of Depression (2ⁿᵈ Ed). New York: Guilford Press.

22. Beck, A.T., Rush, A.J., Shaw, B.F., & Emery, G. (1979). Cognitive therapy of Depression. New York: Guilford Press.

23. Stevens, D.E., Merikangas, K.R., Merikangas, J.R. (1995). Comorbidity of depression and other medical conditions. In E.E. Beckham & W.R. Leber (Eds). Handbook of Depression (2ⁿᵈ Ed). New York: Guilford Press.

24. Maris, R. W. (1992). Overview of the study of suicide assessment and prediction. In Maris, R. W., Berman, A.L., Maltsberger, J.T., & Yufit, R.I. (Eds) (1992). Assessment and prediction of suicide. New York: Guilford Press

25. Peruzzi, N. & Bongar, B. (1999). Assessing risk for completed suicide in patients with major depression: Psychologists' views of critical factors. Professional Psychology: Research and Practice, 30(6), 576-580.

26. Sommers-Flanagan, J. & Sommers-Flanagan, R. (1995). Intake interviewing with suicidal patients: A systematic approach. Professional Psychology: Research and Practice, 26(1), 41-47.

27. Weishaar, M.E., & Beck, A.T. (1992). Clinical and cognitive predictors of suicide. In Maris, R.W., Berman, A.L., Maltsberger, J.T., & Yufit, R.I. (Eds) (1992). Assessment and prediction of suicide. New York: Guilford Press

28. Maris, R.W. (1981). Pathways to suicide: A survey of self-destructive behaviors. Baltimore: John Hopkins University Press.

29. Clark, D. C. (1998). The evaluation and management of the suicidal patient.(In P. M. Kleespies (Ed.), Emergencies in mental health practice: Evaluation and management (pp. 75—94) . New York: Guilford Press.)

30. Kravitz, H.M., & Newman, A.J. (1995). Medical diagnostic procedures for depression: An update from a decade of promise. In E.E. Beckham & W.R. Leber (Eds). Handbook of Depression (2ⁿᵈ Ed). New York: Guilford Press.

31. Koranyi, E. (1979). Morbidity and rate of undiagnosed physical illness in a psychiatric clinic population. Archives of General Psychiatry, 36, 414-419.

32. Hall, R., Popkin, M., Devaul, R., Fallaice, L. & Stickney, S. (1978). Physical illness presenting as psychiatric disease. Archives of General Psychiatry, 35, 1315-1320.

33. Sadek, N., & Nemeroff, C. (2000). Update on the Neurobiology of Depression. CME Medscape: Psychiatry and Mental Health Treatment Updates. Retrieved October 17, 1999 from the World Wide Web: http://www.medscape.com/Medscape/psychiatry/TreatmentUpdate/2000/tu03/public/toc-tu03.html

34. Beutler, L.E. (2000). David and Goliath: When empirical and clinical standards of practice meet. American Psychologist, 55(9), 997-1007.

35. Beutler, L.E. (2000). David and Goliath: When empirical and clinical standards of practice meet. American Psychologist, 55(9), 997-1007.

36. Karau, T.B., Gelenberg, A., Merriam, A., & Wang, P. (2000). Practice guidelines for the treatment of patients with major depressive disorder (Revision). American Journal of Psychiatry, 157(4), (April 2000 Supplement).

37. American Psychiatric Association (1993). Practice guidelines for major depressive disorder in adults. American Journal of Psychiatry, 150 (Suppl. 4), 1-26.

38. Rush, A.J., Golden, W.E., Hall, G.W., Herrera, M., Houston, A., Kathol, R.G., Katon, W., Matchett, C.L., Petty, F., Shulberg, H.C., Smith, G.R., & Stuart, G.W. (1993). Depression in primary care: Vol. 2. Treatment of Major Depression. (AHCPR Publication No. 93-0551). Rockville, MD: U.S. Department of Health and Human Services.

39. Roth, A., & Fonagy, P. (1996). What Works for Whom? A Critical Review of Psychotherapy Research. New York: Guilford Press.

40. Nathan, P.E. & Gorman, J.M. (Eds). (1998). A Guide to Treatments that Work. New York: Oxford University Press.

41. Task Force on Promotion and Dissemination of Psychological Procedures (1995). Training in and dissemination of empirically validated psychological treatments: Report and Recommendations. American Psychologist, 48(1), 3-23.

42. Beutler, L.E., Clarkin, J.F., & Bongar, B. (2000). Guidelines for the Systematic Treatment of the Depressed Patient. New York: Oxford University Press.

43. Getz, M., Pedersen, W.S., Plomin, R., Messelroade, J.R., and McClearn, G.E., (1992). Importance of shared genes and shared environments for symptoms of Depression in older adults. Archives of General Psychiatry, 101, 701-708.

44. Blatt, S.J. (1974). Levels of object representation in anaclitic and introjective Depression. The Psychoanalytic Study of the Child, 29, 107-157.

45. Shapiro, D.A., Barkham, M., Rees, A., Hardy, G.E., Reynolds, S., & Startup, M. (1994). Effects of treatment duration and severity of depression on the effectiveness of cognitive-behavioral and psychodynamic-interpersonal psychotherapy. Journal of Consulting and Clinical Psychology, 62, 522-534.

46. Shapiro, D.A., & Firth, J.A. (1987). Prescriptive vs. exploratory psychotherapy: outcomes of the Sheffield Psychotherapy Project. British Journal of Psychiatry, 151, 790-799.

47. Eysenck, H.C. (1993). Psychoanalysis: Pseudo-science. (Letter to the editor), American Psychological Association Monitor, 24 (8) p. 4.

48. McLean, P.D. & Hakstian, A.R. (1979). Clinical depression: Comparative efficacy of outpatient treatments. Journal of Consulting and Clinical Psychology, 47, 818-836.

49. Giles, T.R. (1993). Handbook of effective psychotherapy. New York: Plenum Press.

50. Rachman, S.J., & Wilson, G.T. (1980). The effects of psychotherapy (2nd ed.). New York: Pergamon Press.

51. Elkin, I., Shea, T., Watkins, J.T., Imber, S.D., Sotsky, S.M., Collins, J.F., Glass, D.R., Pilkonis, P.A., Leber, W.R., Docherty, J.P., Giester, S.J., Parloff, M.B. (1989). National Institute of Mental Health treatment of Depression collaborative research program: General effectiveness of treatments. Archives of General Psychiatry, 46, 971-982.

52. Craighead, W.E., Craighead, L.W., & Ilardi, S.S, (1998). Psychosocial treatments for Major Depressive Disorder. In P.E. Nathan & J.M. Gorman (Eds). A Guide to Treatments that Work. New York: Oxford University Press.

53. Klerman, G., Weissman, M., Rounsaville, B., & Chevron, E. (1984) Interpersonal psychotherapy of Depression. New York: Basic Books.

54. Klerman, G. & Weissman, M. (1993). Interpersonal psychotherapy for depression: Background and concepts. In G.L. Klerman and M.M. Weissman (Eds.) New applications of interpersonal psychotherapy. Washington, DC: American Psychiatric Press.

55. Weissman, M.M., Klerman, G.L., Prusoff, B.A., Sholomskas, D., & Padian, N. (1981). Depressed outpatients: Results one year after treatment with drugs and/or interpersonal psychotherapy. <u>Archives of General Psychiatry, 38</u>, 51-55.

56. Weissman, M.M., Prusoff, B.A., DiMascio, A., Neu, Glokaney, & Klerman, G.L. (1979) The efficacy of drugs and psychotherapy in the treatment of acute depressive episodes. <u>American Journal of Psychiatry, 136</u>, 555-558.

57. Lewinsohn, P.M., Sullivan, J.M., & Grosscup, S.J. (1980). Changing reinforcing events: An approach to the treatment of depression. <u>Psychotherapy: Theory, Research, and Practice, 47</u>. 322-334.

58. Jacobson, N.S., Dobson, K.S., Truax, P.A., Addis, M.E., Koerner, K., Gollan, J.K., Gortner, E. & Prince, S.E. (1996). A component analysis of cognitive-behavioral treatment for depression. <u>Journal of Consulting and Clinical Psychology, 64</u>, 74-80.

59. Yankura, J., and Dryden, W. (1990). <u>Doing RET: Albert Ellis in action.</u> New York: Springer Publishing.

60. Ellis, A. (1976). The biological basis of human irrationality. <u>Journal of Individual Psychology, 32</u>, 145-168.

61. Beck, A.T., & Freeman, A. (1990). <u>Cognitive therapy of personality disorders.</u> New York: Guilford Press.

62. Robins, C.J., & Hayes, A.M. (1993). An appraisal of cognitive therapy. <u>Journal of Consulting and Clinical Psychology, 61</u>, 205-214.

63. Smith, M.L., & Glass, G.V. (1977). Meta-analysis of psychotherapy outcome studies. <u>American Psychologist, 32</u>, 752-760.

64. Lyons, L.C., Woods, P.J. (1991). The efficacy of rational-emotive therapy: A quantitative review of the outcome research. <u>Clinical Psychology Review, 11</u>, 357-369.

65. Hollon, S.D., Shelton, R.C., & Loosen, P.T. (1991). Cognitive therapy and pharmacotherapy for depression. <u>Journal of Consulting and Clinical Psychology, 59</u>, 88-99.

66. Beck. A.T. (1993). Cognitive therapy: Past, present, and future. <u>Journal of Consulting and Clinical Psychology, 61</u>, 194-198.

67. Yalom, I.D. (1983). <u>Inpatient group psychotherapy.</u> New York: Basic Books.

68. Lewinsohn, P.M., Antonuccio, D.O., Breckenridge, J., & Jeri, L. (1984). <u>The Coping with Depression Course: A psychoeducational interview for unipolar Depression.</u> Eugene, OR: Castalia Publishing Co.

69. Luby, J.L., & Yalom, I.D. (1992). Group therapy. In E.S. Paykel (Ed.) (1992). <u>Handbook of Affective Disorders</u> (2nd Ed.). New York: Guilford Press.

70. Yalon, I.D. (1975). <u>The theory and practice of group psychotherapy</u> (2nd Ed.) New York: Basic Books

71. Clarke, G., & Lewinsohn, P.M. (1989). The Coping with Depression Course: A group psychoeducational intervention for unipolar Depression. <u>Behavior Change, 6</u>, 54-69.

72. Shaw, B.F. (1977). Comparison of cognitive therapy and behavior therapy in the treatment of depression. <u>Journal of Consulting and Clinical Psychology, 45</u>, 543-551.

73. Gioe, V.J. (1975). Cognitive modification and positive group experience as a treatment for depression. Doctoral dissertation, Temple University. <u>Dissertation Abstracts International, 36</u>, 3039B-3040B (University microfilms 75-28, 219.)

74. Covi, L., Roth, D., & Lipman, R.S. (1982). Cognitive group psychotherapy of depression: The close-ended group. <u>American Journal of Psychotherapy, 36</u>, 459-460.

75. Paykel, E.S., Myers, J.K., Dienelt, M.N., Klerman, G.L., Lindenthal, J.J., &Pepper, M.P. (1969). Life events and depression: A controlled study. <u>Archives of General Psychiatry, 21</u>, 753-760.

76. Vaughn, C.E., & Leff, J.P. (1976). The influence of family and social factors on the course of psychiatric illness: A comparison of schizophrenic and depressed neurotic patients. British Journal of Psychiatry, 129, 125-137.

77. Merikangas, K.R. (1982). Divorce and assortative mating for psychiatric disorders and psychological traits. Archives of General Psychiatry, 141, 74-76.

78. Gotlib, I.H., & McCabe, S.B. (1990). Marriage and Psychopathology. In F.D. Fincham & T.N. Bradbury (Eds.). The psychology of marriage: Basic issues and applications. New York: Guilford Press.

79. Costello, C.G. (1982). Social factors associated with depression: A retrospective community study. Psychological Medicine, 12, 329-339.

80. Prince, S.E. & Jacobson, N.S. (1995). Couple and family therapy for depression. In E.E. Beckham & W.R. Leber (Eds). Handbook of Depression (2nd Ed). New York: Guilford Press.

81. Carey, G. & Dilalla, D.L. (1994). Personality and psychopathology: Genetic perspective. Journal of Abnormal Psychology, 103, 32-43.

82. Roediger, H.L., Rushton, J.P., Capaldi, E.D., Paris, S.G. (1987). Psychology (2nd ed.). Boston: Little, Brown & Co.

83. Lickey, M.E. & Gordon, B. (1983). Drugs for mental illness: A revolution in psychiatry. New York: W H. Freeman and Co.

84. Kolb, B. & Whishaw, I. (1985). Fundamentals of human neuropsychology (2ndEd.). New York, NY: W.H. Freeman and Co.

85. Nemeroff, C.B. & Schatzberg, A.F. (1998). Pharmacological Treatment of Unipolar Depression. In P.E. Nathan & J.M. Gorman (Eds). A Guide to Treatments that Work. New York: Oxford University Press.

86. Thase, M.E. & Kupfer, D.J. (1996). Recent developments in the pharmacotherapy of mood disorders. Journal of Consulting and Clinical Psychology, 64, 646-659.

87. Albers, L.J., Kahn, R.K., & Reist, C. (2001). Handbook of Psychiatric Drugs. Laguna Hills,CA: Current Clinical Strategies Publishing

88. Akiskal, H.S. (1985). The clinical management of affective disorders. In R. Michels, J.O. Cavenar, K.H. Brodie, A.M. Cooper, S.B. Guze, L.L. Judd, G.L. Klerman, and A.J. Soinit (eds.), Psychiatry, 1, 1-27. Philadelphia: Lippincott.

89. Bortman, A.W., Falk, W.E., and Gelberg, A.J. (1987). Pharmacologic treatment of acute depressive subtypes. In H.Y. Meltzer (Ed.), Psychopharmacology: The third generation of progress (pp. 1031-1040). New York: Raven Press.

90. Frangos, E., Tsitourides, A.S., Psilolignos, P., and Katsanou, N. (1983). Psychotic depressive disorder: A separate entity? Journal of Affective Disorders, 5, 259-265.

91. Antonuccio, D.O. (1993). Psychotherapy vs. medication for depression: Challenging the conventional wisdom. Paper presented at the annual meeting of the American Psychological Association. Toronto, Canada.

92. Steinbreuck, S.M., Maxwell, S.E., & Howard, G.S. (1983). A meta-analysis of psychotherapy and drug therapy in the treatment of unipolar depression with adults. Journal of Consulting and Clinical Psychology, 51, 856-863.

93. Smith, M.L., Glass, G.V., & Miller, T. (1980). The benefits of psychotherapy. Baltimore: John Hopkins University Press.

94. Dobson, K.S. (1989). A meta-analysis of the efficacy of cognitive therapy for depression. Journal of Consulting and Clinical Psychology, 57, 414-419.

95. Conte, H.R., Plutchik, R., Wild, K.V., & Karasu, T.B. (1986). Combined psychotherapy and pharmacotherapy for depression: A systematic analysis of the evidence. Archives of General Psychiatry, 43, 471-479.

96. Hollon, S.D., & Najavits, L. (1988). Review of empirical studies on cognitive therapy. In A.J. Frances, & R.E. Sales (Eds.), American Psychiatric Press Review of Psychiatry, 7, 643-666.

97. Shea, M.T., Elkin, I., Imber, S.D., Sotsky, S.M., Watkins, J.T., Collins, J.F., Pilkonis, P.A., Leber, W.R., Krupnik, J., Dolan, R.T., & Parloff, M.B. (1992). Course of depressive symptoms over follow-up: Findings from the National Institute of Mental Health treatment of depression collaborative research program. Archives of General Psychiatry, 49, 782-787.

98. Evans, M.D., Hollon, S.D., DeRubeis, R.J., Piasecki, J.M., Grove, W.M., Garvey, M.J., & Tuason, V.B. (1992). Differential relapse following cognitive therapy and pharmacotherapy for depression. Archives of General Psychiatry, 49, 802-808.

99. Tkachuk, G.A. & Martin, G.L. (1999). Exercise therapy for patients with psychiatric disorders: Research and clinical implications. Professional Psychology: Research and Practice, 30, 275-282.

100. Bowers, W.A. (1990). Treatment of depressed inpatients: Cognitive therapy plus medication, and medication alone. British Journal of Psychiatry, 130, 201-210.

101. Miller, I.W., Norman, W.H., Keitner, G.I., Bishop, S.G., & Dow, M. (1989). Cognitive-behavioral treatment of depressed inpatients. Behavior Therapy, 20, 25-47.

102. Thase, M.E., Bowler, K., & Harden, T. (1991). Cognitive behavior therapy of endogenous depression: Part 2: Preliminary findings in 16 unmedicated patients. Behavior Therapy, 22, 469-478.

103. Weiner, R.D. (1979). The psychiatric use of electrically induced seizures. American Journal of Psychiatry, 131, 1507-1517.

104. Turek, I.S., & Hanlon, T.P. (1977). The effectiveness and safety of electroconvulsive therapy (ECT). Journal of Nervous and Mental Disease, 164, 419-431.

105. Fink, M. (1978). Efficacy and safety of induced seizures (EST) in man. Comprehensive Psychiatry, 19, 1-18.

106. Fink, M. (1992). Electroconvulsive therapy. In E.S. Paykel (Ed.) Handbook of affective disorders (2nd Ed.). New York: Guilford Press.

107. Avery, D. & Lubrano, A. (1979). Depression treated with imipramine and ECT: The DeCarolis study reconsidered. American Journal of Psychiatry, 136, 559-562.

108. Zung, W. (1965). A self-rating depression scale. Archives of General Psychiatry, 12, 63-70.

109. Radloff, L. (1977). The CES-D scale: A self-report depression scale for research in the general population. Applied Psychological Measurement, 1, 385-401.

110. Santor, D.A., Zuroff, D.C., Ramsay, P.C., & Palacios, J. (1995). Examining scale discriminability in the BDI and the CES-D as a function of depressive severity. Psychological Assessment, 7(2), 131-139.

111. Katz, R., Shaw, B.F., Vallis, T.M., Kaiser, A.S. (1995). The assessment of severity and symptom patterns in depression. In E.E. Beckham & W.R. Leber (Eds). Handbook of Depression (2nd Ed). New York: Guilford Press.

112. Beck, A., Ward, C., Mendelson, M., Mack, J. & Erbaugh, J. (1961). An inventory for measuring depression. Archives of General Psychiatry, 4, 561-571.

113. Carlson, J.F. (1998). Review of Beck Depression Inventory. In J.C. Impara & B.S. Plake (Eds). The Thirteenth Mental Measurements Yearbook. [Number 31, pp.117-119] Lincoln, NE: Buros Institute.

114. Murphy, L.L., Impara, J.C., Plake, B.S. (Eds). <u>Tests in Print V</u>: <u>An Index to Tests, Test Reviews, and the Literature on Specific Tests</u>. [Number 272, p. 79] Lincoln, NE: Buros Institute.

115. Steer, R.A., Beck, A.T., Clark, D.A. & Beck, J.S. (1994). Psychometric properties of the Cognition Checklist with psychiatric outpatients and university students. <u>Psychological Assessment, 6(1),</u> 67-70.

116. Clark, D.A.; Cook, A., & Snow, D. (1998). Depressive symptom differences in hospitalized, medically ill, depressed psychiatric inpatients and nonmedical controls. <u>Journal of Abnormal Psychology, 107(1),</u> 38-48.

117. Brink, T.L., Yesavage, J.A., Lum, O. ** (1982). Screening tests for geriatric depression. <u>Clinical Gerontologist, 1(1),</u> 37-43.

118. Holroyd, S., & Clayton, A. H. (2000). Measuring Depression in the Elderly: Which scale is best? <u>Medscape Mental Health, 5</u>(5). Retrieved September 26, 2000 from the World Wide Web: http://psychiatry.medscape.com/Medscape/psychiatry/journal/2000/v05.n05/mh3033.holr

119. Alexopoulous, G.S., Abrams, R.C., Young, R.C., & Shamoian, C.A.(1988). Cornell Scale for Depression in Dementia. <u>Biological Psychiatry, 23(3),</u> 271-284.

120. Coyne, J. (1994). Self-reported distress: Analog or ersatz Depression? <u>Psychological Bulletin. 116</u> (1), 29-45.

121. Fechner-Bates, S., Coyne, J., & Schwenk, T. (1994). The relationship of self-reported distress to depressive disorders and other psychopathology. <u>Journal of Consulting and Clinical Psychology, 62</u>, 550-559.

122. Hamilton, M. (1960). A rating scale for depression. <u>Journal of Neurology and Neurosurgical Psychiatry, 12</u>, 56-62.

123. Kobak, K.A., Reynolds, W.M., Rosenfeld, R. & Greist, J.H. (1990). Development and validation of a computer-administered version of the Hamilton Depression Rating Scale. <u>Psychological Assessment, 2(1),</u> 56-63.

124. Reynolds, W.M., Kobak, K.A. (1995). Reliability and validity of the Hamilton Depression Inventory: A paper-and-pencil version of the Hamilton Depression Rating Scale Clinical Interview. <u>Psychological Assessment, 7(4),</u> 472-483.

125. Brown, C., Schulberg, H.C., Madonia, M.J. (1995). Assessment depression in primary care practice with the Beck Depression Inventory and the Hamilton Rating Scale for Depression. <u>Psychological Assessment, 7(1),</u> 59-65.

126. First, M., Spitzer, L., Gibbon, M. & Williams, J. (1995). <u>Structured Clinical Interview for Axis I DSM-IV Disorders (SCID Version 2.0)</u>. Washington, DC: American Psychiatric Press.

127. Endicott, J. (1986). Schedule for Affective Disorders and Schizophrenia, Regular and Change versions: Measure of depression. In N. Sartorius & T.A. Ban (Eds). <u>Assessment of Depression</u>. Heidelberg: Springer-Verlag.

128. Hasin, D.L., & Grant, B.F. (1987). Diagnosing depressive disorders in patients with alcohol and drug problems: A comparison of the SADS-L and the DIS. <u>Journal of Psychiatric Research, 21</u> (3), 301-311.

129. Robins, L.N., Cottler, L., Bucholz, K. (1995). <u>Diagnostic Interview Schedule for DSM-IV,</u> St. Louis: Washington University.

130. Blouin, A.G., Perez, E.L., & Blouin, J.H. (1988). Computerized administration of the Diagnostic Interview Schedule. <u>Psychiatry Research, 22</u> (3), 335-344.

131. Robins, L.N., Wing, J., Wittchen, H.U., Helzer, J.E., Babor, T.F., Burke, J., Farmer, A. Jablenski, A., Pickens, R., Regier, D.A., Sartorius, N. & Towle, L.H. (1988). The Composite International Diagnostic Interview: An epidemiologic instrument suitable for use in conjunction with different diagnostic systems and in different cultures. <u>Archives of General Psychiatry, 45</u>, 1069-1077.

132. World Health Organization (1997). Composite International Diagnostic Interview Schedule for DSM-IV, Version 2.1, Geneva: World Health Organization.

133. Whooley, M.A., Avins, A.I., Miranda, J. & Browner, W.S. (1997). Case-finding instruments for depression: Two questions are as good as many. Journal of General Internal Medicine, 12, 439-445.

134. Brody, D.S., Hahn, S.R., Spitzer, R.L., Kroenke, K., Linzer, M., deGruy, F.V., & Williams, J.B. (1998). Identifying patients with depression in primary care settings: A more efficient method. Archives of Internal Medicine, 158, 2469 - 2475.

135. Spitzer, R.L., Kroenke, K., & Williams, J.B. (1999). Validation and utility of the self-report version of the PRIME-MD: The PHQ Primary Care Study. Journal of the American Medical Association, 282, 1737.

136. Baer, L., Jacobs, D.G., Meszler-Reizes, J., Blais, M., Fava, M., Kessler, R., Magruder, K., Murphy, J., Kopans, B., Cukor, P., Leahy, L., O'Laughlen, J. (2000). Development of a brief screening instrument: The HANDS. Psychotherapy and Psychosomatics, 69(1), 35-41.

137. Fernandez, E. (1998). Review of Beck Hopelessness Scale. In J.C. Impara & B.S. Plake (Eds). The Thirteenth Mental Measurements Yearbook. [Number 32, pp.123-124] Lincoln, NE: Buros Institute.

138. Fernandez, E. (1998). Review of Beck Scale of Suicidal Ideation. In J.C. Impara & B.S. Plake (Eds). The Thirteenth Mental Measurements Yearbook. [Number 33, pp.125-126] Lincoln, NE: Buros Institute.

139. Stewart, J.R. (1998). Review of Beck Scale of Suicidal Ideation. In J.C. Impara & B.S. Plake (Eds). The Thirteenth Mental Measurements Yearbook. [Number 33, pp.126-127] Lincoln, NE: Buros Institute.

140. Golding, S.L. (1985). Review of Suicide Probability Scale. In J.V. Mitchell, Jr. (Ed). The Ninth Mental Measurements Yearbook, Vol. II. Lincoln, NE: Buros Institute.

141. Exner, J.E. (1993). The Rorschach: A comprehensive system; volume 1: basic foundations. Somerset, New Jersey: John Wiley and Sons.

142. Hathaway, S.R., & McKinley, J.C. (1983). The Minnesota Multiphasic Personality Inventory manual. New York: Psychological Corporation.

143. Hathaway, S.R., Butcher, J.N., & McKinley, J.C. (1989). Minnesota Multiphasic Personality Inventory—2. Minneapolis, MN: University of Minnesota Press.

144. Graham, J.R. (1990). MMPI-2: Assessing personality and psychopathology. New York: Oxford University Press.

Index

© Compact Clinicals

Compact Clinicals

Ordering in three easy steps:

1 **Please fill out completely:**

Billing/Shipping Information

Individual/Company   Department/Mail Stop
_____

Profession
_____

Street Address/P.O. Box
_____

City, State, Zip
_____

Telephone   ☐ Ship to residence   ☐ Ship to business

2 **Here's what I'd like to order:**

Book Name	Book Qty.	Unit Price	Total
Aggressive and Defiant Behavior The Latest Assessment and Treatment Strategies for the Conduct Disorders		$14.95	
Attention Deficit Hyperactivity Disorder (in Adults and Children) The Latest Assessment and Treatment Strategies		$14.95	
Borderline Personality Disorder The Latest Assessment and Treatment Strategies		$14.95	
Depression in Adults The Latest Assessment and Treatment Strategies		$14.95	
Obsessive Compulsive Disorder The Latest Assessment and Treatment Strategies		$14.95	
Post-Traumatic Stress Disorder The Latest Assessment and Treatment Strategies		$14.95	
		Subtotal	
		Tax Add (6.85% in MO)	
		Shipping Fee Add ($3.75 for the first book and $1.00 for each additional book)	
		Total Amount	

Continuing Education credits available for mental health professionals. Call 1-800-408-8830 for details.

3 **Payment Method:** Telephone Orders/Toll Free: 1(800)408-8830 • Fax Orders to: 1(816)587-7198
Send Postal Orders to: Compact Clinicals • 7205 NW Waukomis Dr., Suite A • Kansas City, MO 64151
    ☐ Check Enclosed
    ☐ Please charge to my:
        ○ Visa   Name on Card   _____
        ○ MasterCard   Cardholder Signature   _____
        ○ Discover Card   Account #/Exp. Date   _ _ _ _ - _ _ _ _ - _ _ _ _ - _ _ _ _ (_ _/_ _)

We Want Your Opinion!

Comments about the book: _____
Name of Book

_____

_____

_____

_____

Other titles you want Compact Clinicals to offer:

_____

_____

_____

_____

Please provide your name and address in the space below to be placed on our mailing list.

_____

_____

_____

_____

 **Compact Clinicals**

Ordering in three easy steps:

1 **Please fill out completely:**

Billing/Shipping Information

Individual/Company _____ Department/Mail Stop _____

Profession _____

Street Address/P.O. Box _____

City, State, Zip _____

Telephone _____ ☐ Ship to residence ☐ Ship to business

2 **Here's what I'd like to order:**

Book Name	Book Qty.	Unit Price	Total
Aggressive and Defiant Behavior The Latest Assessment and Treatment Strategies for the Conduct Disorders		$14.95	
Attention Deficit Hyperactivity Disorder (in Adults and Children) The Latest Assessment and Treatment Strategies		$14.95	
Borderline Personality Disorder The Latest Assessment and Treatment Strategies		$14.95	
Depression in Adults The Latest Assessment and Treatment Strategies		$14.95	
Obsessive Compulsive Disorder The Latest Assessment and Treatment Strategies		$14.95	
Post-Traumatic Stress Disorder The Latest Assessment and Treatment Strategies		$14.95	
		Subtotal	
		Tax Add (6.85% in MO)	
		Shipping Fee Add ($3.75 for the first book and $1.00 for each additional book)	
		Total Amount	

Continuing Education credits available for mental health professionals. Call 1-800-408-8830 for details.

3 **Payment Method:** Telephone Orders/Toll Free: 1(800)408-8830 • Fax Orders to: 1(816)587-7198
Send Postal Orders to: Compact Clinicals • 7205 NW Waukomis Dr., Suite A • Kansas City, MO 64151
☐ Check Enclosed
☐ Please charge to my:
○ Visa   Name on Card _____
○ MasterCard   Cardholder Signature _____
○ Discover Card Account #/Exp. Date _ _ _ _ - _ _ _ _ - _ _ _ _ - _ _ _ _ (_ _/_ _)